CW01499688

"This age-appropriate biograph[...] compelling and well-written for [...] Corrie's testimony of courage, sacrifice, and hope will spur kids on to see the life-changing power of living radically for Jesus in even the darkest moments of life."

Sarah Walton, author, *The Long Road Home*; coauthor, *Hope When It Hurts*

"Corrie ten Boom's remarkable story of faith, perseverance, and forgiveness has encouraged generations. Now Jennifer Kelley brings the riches of this story to young readers in a heartfelt and poignant biography. Kelley sensitively handles the tragedies in Corrie's life as she highlights God's provision and mercy in the darkest of moments. Children who dive into these pages will find an accessible, engaging, and moving account that will inspire their minds and shape their hearts for years to come."

Kathryn Butler, author, The Dream Keeper Saga and *The Storyteller's Bible*

"Every child should read the compelling story of Corrie ten Boom. A true hero of the faith, she survived the Nazi death camps to tell the story of Christ's triumph over the worst evil. This beautifully illustrated, creatively told biography will inspire similar courage in this generation. Make sure this book is in your home."

Daniel Darling, Director, Land Center for Cultural Engagement; author, *The Characters of Christmas*; *Jesus and the Characters of Christmas*; and *The Dignity Revolution*

The Story of Corrie ten Boom

Lives of Faith and Grace

Edited by Champ Thornton

Lives of Faith and Grace

The Story of Corrie ten Boom

The Watchmaker Who Forgave Her Enemies

Jennifer T. Kelley

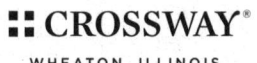

WHEATON, ILLINOIS

The Story of Corrie ten Boom: The Watchmaker Who Forgave Her Enemies
© 2025 by Jennifer Thornton Kelley
Illustrations © Crossway
Published by Crossway
        1300 Crescent Street
        Wheaton, Illinois 60187
All rights reserved. No part of this publication may be reproduced, stored
in a retrieval system, or transmitted in any form by any means, electronic,
mechanical, photocopy, recording, or otherwise, without the prior
permission of the publisher, except as provided for by USA copyright
law. Crossway® is a registered trademark in the United States of America.
Cover and interior illustrations: T. Lively Fluharty
First printing 2025
Printed in the United States of America
Scripture quotations are from the ESV® Bible (The Holy Bible, English
Standard Version®), © 2001 by Crossway, a publishing ministry of Good
News Publishers. Used by permission. All rights reserved. The ESV text
may not be quoted in any publication made available to the public by a
Creative Commons license. The ESV may not be translated into any other
language.
All emphases in Scripture quotations have been added by the author.
Trade paperback ISBN: 978-1-4335-8349-0
ePub ISBN: 978-1-4335-8352-0
PDF ISBN: 978-1-4335-8350-6

Library of Congress Cataloging-in-Publication Data
Names: Kelley, Jennifer T. (Jennifer Thornton), 1980- author.
Title: The story of Corrie ten Boom: the watchmaker who forgave her enemies / Jennifer
    T. Kelley.
Description: Wheaton, Illinois: Crossway, [2024] | Series: Lives of faith and grace |
    Includes bibliographical references. | Audience: Ages 8–13 | Audience: Grades 4–6
Identifiers: LCCN 2024004820 (print) | LCCN 2024004821 (ebook) | ISBN 9781433583490
    (trade paperback) | ISBN 9781433583506 (PDF) | ISBN 9781433583520 (ePub)
Subjects: LCSH: Ten Boom, Corrie—Juvenile literature. | Christian Biography—
    Netherlands—Juvenile literature. | Missionaries—Netherlands—Biography—Juvenile
    literature. | Missionaries—Germany—Biography—Juvenile literature. | Holocaust,
    Jewish (1939–1945)—Juvenile literature.
Classification: LCC BR1725.T35 K45 2024 (print) | LCC BR1725.T35 (ebook) | DDC
    269/.2092 [B]—dc23/eng/20240226
LC record available at https://lccn.loc.gov/2024004820
LC ebook record available at https://lccn.loc.gov/2024004821

Crossway is a publishing ministry of Good News Publishers.

VP		34	33	32	31	30	29	28	27	26	25
15	14	13	12	11	10	9	8	7	6	5	4	3	2	1

For my sisters:
Christina and April.
You lead with beauty and strength,
and like Corrie's sisters,
your lives point people to Jesus.

"Never be afraid to trust an unknown future to a known God."

CORRIE TEN BOOM

Contents

1

The Face in the Crowd

1947

CORRIE TEN BOOM'S train arrived at the station in Munich. But it was not her first time in Germany. She had been there before.

Just three years earlier, World War II was raging across Europe. At the age of fifty-two, Corrie had been forced to leave her beloved Holland. She and her sister Betsie were packed into train cars with hundreds of other prisoners. They had all been arrested and sentenced. They were being relocated to a German prison camp, to Ravensbrück.

She and Betsie had heard of this camp and its unnamable fears. The barbed wire fences. The cruel guards with guns. The rows of prisoners who were led away never to return.

But that was then.

Now the war was over; it had been three years. And Corrie was no longer a prisoner. She was returning to the war-torn country of Germany to spread the message of God's love and forgiveness.

Now in Munich, Corrie made her way to a German church. A small crowd gathered in the basement to hear her. Rows of wooden chairs creaked as men and women settled in to listen to her incredible story. She stepped to the front, opened her Bible, breathed deeply, and looked around the room. All across the congregation, she saw tired and desperate people.

Her message was simple—"Everyone has sinned, but God will forgive those sins. And when God forgives sins, he does not remember them. It is as if he had thrown them into the bottom of the ocean, never to be seen again!"

When she finished her lesson, the meeting was over. People gathered their belongings and moved toward the back door. Everyone moved. Except one man.

She hadn't noticed him before. He wore a gray coat and carried a brown hat. And he began to walk toward the front. Toward her. He was large with thinning hair and unmistakable blue-gray eyes.

It was then that Corrie *really* saw him. And her mind raced to another place and another time, three years before.

Instead of the gray coat and brown hat, she could see his blue military uniform and the skull and crossbones on his hat. She saw his face as she arrived at Ravensbrück prison. She once again felt the chaos and fear of her arrival there. She could smell sickness

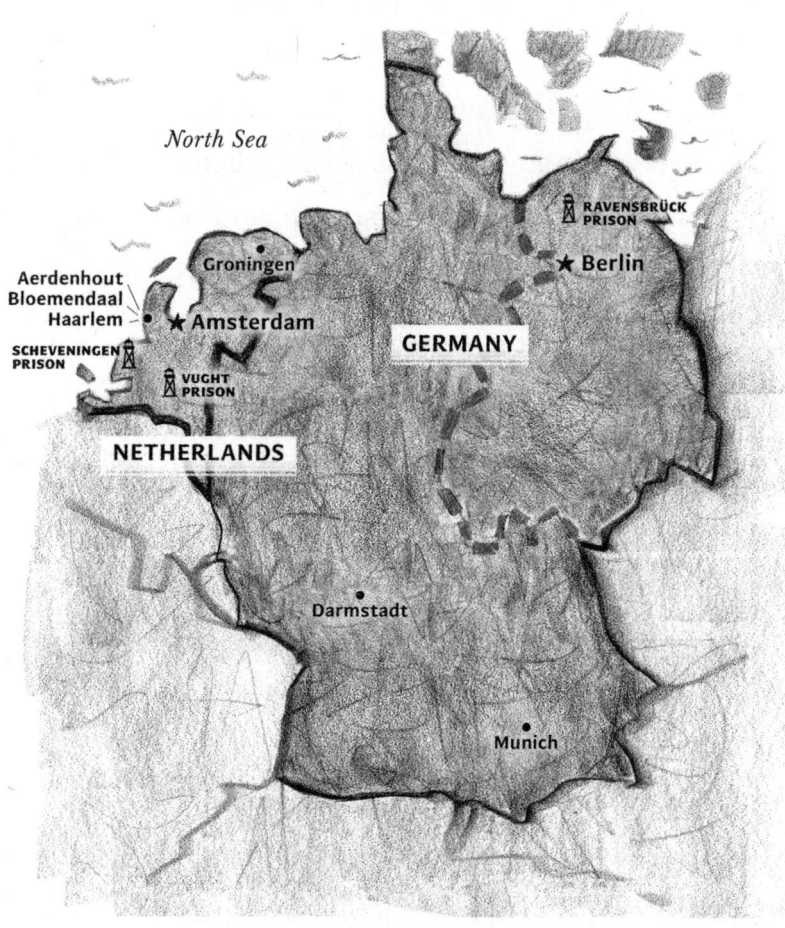

— THE NETHERLANDS AND GERMANY DURING
CORRIE'S LIFETIME (1892–1983) —

Aerdenhout: OUR-den-howt

Amsterdam: AM-ster-dam

Berlin: Bur-LIN

Bloemendaal: BLOOM-en-doll

Darmstadt: DARM-schaht

Groningen: HROW-ni-gen

Haarlem: HAR-lim

Munich: MEW-nik

Ravensbrück Prison:
RAV-ens-brook

Scheveningen Prison:
SHAY-vi-ning-en

Vught Prison: vooft

After World War II, Germany was divided into two—West Germany (with a democratic government) and East Germany (with a Communist government). A dotted line shows this border.

and death all around. A guard was yelling. Terrified prisoners huddled in the corner. And he, the cruelest of the guards, stood watch over it all. A look of hatred on his face.

All this she remembered in a moment.

And now in the basement of this small church, the face of that cruelest guard from that horrible concentration camp appeared once more. Why was he here?

As he walked toward her, she couldn't pull away her eyes. That face. But something wasn't right; something was different. He was smiling.

She heard him speak; a voice she knew too well, "A fine message, Fraulein."

What does he want? Corrie wondered.

"How good it is to know that, as you say, all our sins are at the bottom of the sea! You mentioned Ravensbrück in your talk. I was a guard there. But since that time, I have become a Christian. I know that God has forgiven me for the cruel things I did there."

Corrie's pulse raced. And his next words landed like a bomb.

"But I would like to hear it from your lips as well. Fraulein, . . . will you forgive me?"

Corrie couldn't look at his face. Hatred for him swelled in her heart.

Hadn't he been the cruelest of the prison guards when she arrived? The worst! She remembered the pain. The prisoners' screams. The guard's laughter.

She kept her eyes down. Her hands fiddled with her purse.

No, she would not forgive him. *Impossible!*

The man in the gray coat extended a large hand toward Corrie. "Will you forgive me?"

He may have stood there with his hand outstretched for only a moment. But time slowed down for Corrie. Yes, she had taught about loving and forgiving others. But could she herself forgive this man? This awful guard who had treated her and others so cruelly?

Her whole life had led to this moment. Her whole life had prepared her for what she should say.

But how could she? How can you forgive the unforgivable?

2

Small Beginnings

1892–1909

ON GOOD FRIDAY, April 15, 1892, in the city of Amsterdam, Netherlands, Cornelia Arnolda Johanna ten Boom was born. What a big name for such a little baby!

Corrie, as everyone called her, had been born a month early and was clinging to life. Her parents,

Casper and Cor, had three older children Betsie (age seven), Willem (age six), and Nollie (age one and a half). Only a few years before, their six-month-old son (Hendrik) had died. And now their new baby was tiny and weak. Her skin was bluish white. And many of the Ten Booms' family and friends thought she might not survive.

However, Corrie's papa and mama believed in the power of prayer, because they were devoted Christians. So the whole family began to pray, and God heard their prayers. Soon Corrie began to grow, and before long the weak baby had grown into a smart, funny, and determined little girl with dark wavy hair. She loved playing with her doll, who she named Casperina (in honor of her dad, Casper). And she and Nollie loved to ice-skate on the frozen canals and jump rope in the street near their house. When Corrie was still young, her family moved from the busy city of Amsterdam to her papa's small hometown: Haarlem. The winding streets of Haarlem curved along narrow canals and beside tall windmills and ancient brick buildings. St. Bavos, the old cathedral, towered over the city square, and skinny brick streets branched off the square in every direction. Shops and homes lined the curving streets. And just a few minutes' walk from the city square sat the Ten Boom watch shop (*Horlogerie ten Boom* in Dutch). The shop had belonged to their family since Corrie's grandfather Willem opened the business in 1837.

The shop faced the street with small alleys running alongside and behind it. And Corrie's family lived in the two floors above the shop. New watches and clocks of different sizes glistened from the window displays. The shop was little, nothing like the big fancy shops in Amsterdam, 20 miles away.

The Ten Booms gave their home a name: the Beje (pronounced *BAY-yay*). This nickname was taken from the much longer name of their street: Barteljorisstraat (Bar-tol-YOR-uh-strot). The two floors above the shop soon became too full to accommodate the whole Ten Boom family—Corrie's parents, two sisters, one brother, and three aunts (her mother's sisters): Aunt

Bep, Aunt Jans, and Aunt Anna. So Papa bought the tall skinny house across the tiny alley behind the shop. The family enclosed the space between the buildings and added a staircase that spiraled between the

— The Beje —

The Beje consisted of two tall houses joined together by a winding staircase. The first floor of the original home held both the watch shop and a small workroom. The second floor had two rooms too. The first was a tiny bedroom (originally Aunt Jans's, but later Betsie's room). And the second room was the sitting room where the family spent time together talking, reading, and playing piano. The third floor had a bathroom and four small bedrooms. These bedrooms were originally Aunt Anna's, Aunt Bep's, Willem's, and Betsie's rooms. But later these bedrooms were used to house the Ten Booms' foster children and any other guests who stayed at the Beje.

two parts of the now-combined house. The staircase started at the first floor. And it ended on the top floor where Nollie and Corrie shared a room. But the three floors of the narrow original house did not align with

A winding staircase ran between the original house and the skinny house behind it. This house had four floors. The bottom floor was the cellar. The next floor held the dining room and a tiny kitchen. The third floor held Papa and Mama's room and another bathroom. And on the top floor was a bedroom that Corrie and Nollie shared.

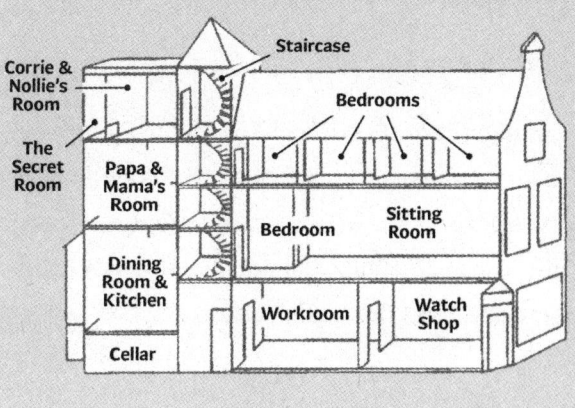

— A Dive into Dutch —

Hallo **(HEH-low)** = hello

Tot Ziens **(TOT-zeens)** = goodbye

Straat **(strot)** = street

Huis **(hows)** = house

Kerk **(kurk)** = church

Horloge **(hor-LOW-zhuh)** = watch

Horlogerie **(hor-LOW-zher-ee)** = watchmaking

Klok **(klok)** = clock

Fiets **(feetz)** = bicycle

Gezellig **(heh-SELL-ick)** = The Dutch word *gezel* means "companionship." But there is no English word for *gezellig*. The closest translation is "cozy, inviting, and friendly." Many people say that *gezellig* best describes the Dutch culture.

the four floors of the small skinny house behind it. As Corrie grew up, she came to love the Beje, the funny, unique, and lopsided little house that she called home.

Corrie was five years old on her first day of school. She stood at the bottom of the spiral stairs, her fingers wrapped around the handrail. She had decided that she did not need school. She already knew how to read, so she should just stay home and learn all she needed from Mama, Papa, and Aunt Anna. Plus, Casperina needed her!

Her papa gently unwrapped her fingers from the staircase railing. He held her hand and walked her down the street to her school. Shopkeepers and people on bicycles watched as Corrie walked and cried.

When they arrived, Corrie saw another little boy crying and being carried by his father. *At least I was walking!* she thought. Corrie realized what a silly girl she was being and stopped crying on the spot. Her papa leaned down, kissed her forehead, and assured her that he would be there when she came home that afternoon. And, of course, he was.

Corrie's parents were glad that Corrie learned to enjoy school. And they also were happy to teach their children to know God. Just as Corrie's grandfather had done, every evening Corrie's father gathered the family after dinner to read the Bible and pray. And as they prayed, Corrie's family always remembered to pray for a special group of people: the Jews. (The Ten Booms had been praying for the Jewish people ever since Corrie's grandfather had been a young man.) And every Sunday morning, like clockwork, Corrie's family attended church at St. Bavos. On some evenings, the Ten Booms would walk to the cathedral for concerts and Bible classes.

Corrie loved church, and she loved to read and play too. One day while playing with her dolls, Corrie knocked on a make-believe door. She was sad that no one answered her knocking. Watching her play, her mama told Corrie that just like someone knocking on a door, Jesus was asking to come into Corrie's heart.

Corrie knew that Jesus is God's Son. Jesus loved her and had come to rescue her from her sins. And

Jesus wanted Corrie to know him, to trust him, and to love him. Even though she was still young, she understood the gospel and wanted Jesus to be her Savior.

Corrie replied, "Yes, Mama, I want Jesus in my heart."

As Corrie grew up, she wanted others to know about Jesus too. As she walked and played in the

streets near her house, she saw men and women who loved sin more than God. They didn't know the Bible, and they didn't know Jesus. And just a block away from the Beje stood the police station and jail with its prisoners. *How sad must the prisoners be!* Corrie thought. So she decided to pray for them. And she did—for years—even though she wasn't quite sure if any of her prayers would ever be answered. Corrie later said, "Never doubt whether God hears our prayers, even the unusual ones."

Corrie quickly grew up. She was no longer a sickly little girl. Instead, she graduated from her high school, took theology classes, sewed, cooked, played the piano, and learned to speak three languages— German, English, and, of course, Dutch. She also continued praying and caring for people in need.

As a young adult, Corrie loved her old lopsided house. It wasn't fancy, but it was always full—for even a crooked smile can reveal a happy heart.

For now, the Beje was full of family and laughter, of prayer, of music, and of people who came for help.

It had been that way long before Corrie was born, and it would continue even as Corrie grew up. But no one could imagine what lay ahead for her family, their watch shop, and their unusual house.

Being a Somebody

1910–1939

WHEN CORRIE GRADUATED from her high school, she began to dream of what her future would hold. She wanted to do something. She wanted to be somebody!

So when a wealthy family with a young daughter offered her a full-time nanny position, Corrie gladly accepted. This family's large, luxurious home sat on the shore of the North Sea. Although only 10 miles from Haarlem, Corrie soon realized that it was a world away from all that she had ever known. The Beje, though little, was *gezellig*, full of love and laughter. And while this new house was large, it was lifeless and very lonely.

A few months later, Corrie received news from the Beje: her Aunt Bep had died and her mother was sick. Corrie returned home for the funeral. Her mama needed help, and her elderly Aunt Anna and Aunt Jans needed someone young who could help care for them too.

Corrie had seen the world outside the Beje. She had enjoyed her independence, but now she was ready to be home where she was needed.

She returned to the Beje to cook, clean, and care for her family. But everything seemed different now, and more difficult. One evening while sitting with her father at the oval dining table, Corrie felt especially sad and stressed. *Mama was getting weaker, business in the shop was slow, and bills needed to be paid. What were they going to do?* She stared blankly at the red and black checkered tablecloth.

Papa looked at Corrie. His long beard covered his kind face. He could tell something was worrying his daughter. "Don't forget, Corrie—underneath us are the everlasting arms. We won't fall." He then quoted Deuteronomy 33:27:

> The eternal God is your dwelling place,
>   and underneath are the everlasting arms.

Papa knew his Bible! And he knew how to give comfort and speak God's truth. Corrie would remember her father's words, even as life soon changed for her whole family and for their country.

When Corrie was twenty-two years old, war broke out in Europe. (This war would later be called "The Great War" or "World War I.") German troops invaded France, Russia, and other surrounding countries, but not the Netherlands. Instead, the Netherlands remained neutral. And from the safety of the Beje, the Ten Booms prayed for the people facing danger.

— One Country, Two Names —

Have you noticed that Corrie's home country has two names: the Netherlands *and* Holland? The official name of the country is "the Kingdom of the Netherlands" or "The Netherlands" (which means "lower countries" or "low-lying lands"). Most of the nation is below sea level, so that name just fits!

The name *Holland* actually refers to two western regions in the Netherlands (North Holland and South Holland). But for hundreds of years, people have called the whole country both Holland and the Netherlands.

And interestingly, the people from Holland and the Netherlands aren't called "Hollanders" or "Netherlandians." Instead, they are called *Dutch*. And Dutch is also the language they speak. So Dutch people speak Dutch.

Because her father was the chairman of the International Watchmakers, he knew many German watchmakers. These men had families who might get hurt by the fighting. So after praying for wisdom, Papa made a plan. He and watchmakers all over Holland invited children of German watchmakers to escape and take refuge in their own homes. Because Corrie's brother Willem had gotten married and moved away, the Beje had two empty rooms. So even though there wasn't much money, the Ten Booms opened the Beje as a safe place for many German children during the war.

All during World War I, Corrie and her oldest sister Betsie worked for their family. Nollie got married, but neither Corrie nor Betsie married or moved away. Betsie worked alongside their papa in the shop taking care of bills and paperwork. And Corrie managed the house. She found adventure in cooking and cleaning, and she often set a timer to see how fast she could get her housework done. If she finished before the timer sounded, she rewarded herself with extra time curled up with a book.

After World War I ended, the German children went home to their own families. But the Ten Booms continued to open their home to those in need. This time to children of foreign missionaries. At one point they had seven children staying with them in the Beje. It wasn't always easy, but Corrie, Betsie, and their father loved the noise and excitement that these children brought to the house.

In 1918, Corrie's mother had a stroke and became unable to speak. Corrie later said that even though her mama could not talk, her "love and patience spoke louder than any sermon." Corrie, Betsie, and their father cared for her, and after three years, she died. Corrie later remembered her papa saying that it was the saddest day of his life. Yet, in his grief, he remained grateful. He prayed, "Thank You, Lord, for giving her to me."

When Corrie was twenty-eight years old, her work started to spread beyond the house. Betsie came down with the flu, so Corrie took her place in the shop and began repairing watches. And even though

Corrie felt clumsy at such detailed repairs, like she "had two left hands," she loved the work. One day she asked her father—"Will you teach me the trade of watchmaking?"

Her papa smiled, "Of course I can teach you—and after some time, I will send you to Switzerland to work as an apprentice in a factory. I hope you will become a better watchmaker than I am." Soon Corrie had completed *two* internships in

— The Church Walk Club —

Corrie found joy in teaching. For many years she taught children's Sunday school. And she led Bible classes for people with disabilities. When she was thirty-three years old, she created a Bible club for teenage girls in Haarlem. She called it "The Church Walk Club." The girls in this club met Corrie at 8:30 a.m. on Sunday mornings to play games and walk to church together.

The group of girls grew. So a wealthy Haarlem family donated one of their empty homes to be a clubhouse. Corrie renamed the group the "Haarlem Girls' Clubs" (later called "The Girl Guides").

Switzerland and returned to work alongside her father. Most watchmakers during that time were men, but at the age of thirty-two, Corrie became the first woman in the Netherlands to be a licensed watchmaker.

Corrie began hosting special clubs each night of the week. She and the other leaders taught music, sewing, embroidery, folk dance, catechisms, gymnastics, and English lessons. And every time the club met, one of the leaders taught a short lesson from the Bible.

The club members marched in the yearly Haarlem parade celebrating Queen Wilhelmina's birthday. And in the summers, Corrie and over sixty girls went camping together. The girls loved listening to Corrie's stories around the campfire and hearing her sing to them at bedtime. Through the years, many of the club girls put their faith in Jesus.

And just like the clocks in the shop, time continued to tick on. Years went by. Aunt Jans and Aunt Anna died. The missionary children left the Beje to go to college, begin careers, and get married. And Willem and Nollie had families of their own. Willem and his wife, Tine, had four children: two girls and two boys. And Nollie and her husband, Flip, had six children: three girls and three boys. And with so many changes, Corrie found that she had more time to help others.

When she was young, Corrie had wanted adventure, to do something, to be somebody. Yet she realized that all the excitement—all the big challenges she had hoped for—could be found all around her in everyday life. Real adventure was following Jesus and serving those in need. Corrie later testified that "God's love and power is available to us in the trivial things of everyday life."

By 1939 the Beje was quiet once more. Only Corrie, Betsie, and their elderly father sat around the table. The dining room clock ticked steadily and softly, but the world around them was stirring with winds of war.

Before long, these violent blasts would beat against the Beje door, bringing difficulty and need. And as always, the Ten Booms would answer the door.

4

The Invasion

September 1939–November 1941

ON SEPTEMBER 1, 1939, war began to sweep across
Europe. The German Army, under the evil control
of Nazi leader Adolf Hitler, invaded Poland. This act
of aggression marked the beginning of what became
World War II (WWII). During World War I, only
twenty-five years earlier, Holland had been able to

remain neutral. But this war was different. Before the sun rose on May 10, 1940, the Nazi German military attacked Holland. Families across the country were awakened to the sound of explosions; and fighter planes roared through the skies.

Corrie and Betsie woke up to the sounds of airplanes and artillery. They made their way to the sitting room and peeked out the windows, watching the dark

— Groups in Holland During the Nazi Occupation —

• **Nazi** refers to the German political party led by Adolf Hitler from 1921 to 1945. The Nazis believed that the best people came from the northern European countries, like Germany. But they hated other groups of people they thought inferior (for example, Jewish people, people with disabilities, and anyone who didn't have light-colored skin). The Nazis arrested and killed millions of these people during World War II. The Nazis also hated the Bible. So they confiscated and burned Bibles, along with other books.

- The **Gestapo** were the "Secret State Police" of the Nazi regime. This group arrested people who opposed the Nazi beliefs.

- **NSB** stands for "National Socialist Bond." This was a group of Dutch citizens who supported or worked with the Nazi government. Some Dutch people joined the NSB because they loved the Nazis. And some Dutch people joined simply because they could get extra food.

- The **Underground** or **Dutch Underground** referred to organized groups of Dutch people who secretly undermined and resisted the Nazi government. (That's why it can also be called the Dutch Resistance movement.) They rejected the Nazi ideas so thoroughly that they were willing to risk their lives to break the laws of the Nazi government.

sky turn red. But their elderly father stayed sound asleep. The sisters knelt beside their piano bench to pray. They prayed for Queen Wilhelmina, for their fellow Dutchmen, and for the wounded. Corrie later recalled that "Betsie began to pray for the Germans, up there in the planes, soldiers caught in the fist of the giant evil loose in Germany." Betsie had always been full of compassion and hope—*too full*, thought Corrie. So she prayed, "Oh Lord, . . . listen to Betsie, not me, because I cannot pray for those men at all."

During the next days of fighting, city after city fell to the Nazi army. The Ten Booms listened to nightly radio broadcasts for news about the invasion. Then after a week of fighting, on May 17—the day before her papa's eighty-first birthday—Holland surrendered, and the Nazis took over. Like rats released from a cage, Nazi soldiers swarmed the cities. Their trucks and tanks filled the narrow streets. The dark days of the Nazi occupation had begun.

Soon the Nazis seized control of the government and placed heavy restrictions on the Dutch people.

The officials disconnected the telephone lines and demanded a nightly curfew. People all across the Netherlands had to be inside their homes by 9 p.m. And once the sun went down, they were required to put blackout paper in their windows.

The new government then took control of the media. Dutch newspapers solely featured articles supporting the Nazi government. And then the government demanded that all Dutch citizens surrender their radios. Since the Ten Boom family owned two radios, they chose to hand over only one of them. Corrie carried their small radio to the department store collection site. However, her family carefully hid the larger one in a concealed compartment inside the staircase. If they kept the radio volume low, and someone played the piano very loudly, they could listen to British news reports about the war. Since the Ten Booms still had a radio, more friends and neighbors came to the watch shop—not to buy watches but to hear the news. And many also came to find comfort and to pray with Corrie's father.

As the German occupation stretched into months, the restrictions grew more difficult. One Sunday while the Ten Booms attended church, soldiers entered the cathedral and arrested all the adult men under forty years old. These Dutchmen were seized and sent to Germany as enslaved labor. Many never returned. But the young men were not the only ones in danger. For several years Jews who lived in Germany had been facing arrest, beatings, and even

death. And by 1941 in Nazi-occupied countries such as Holland, the Jewish people began facing the same savage treatment. And it wasn't just the Gestapo who mistreated the Jews; even some of the Dutch people hated their Jewish neighbors and joined the NSB.

On one of their daily walks through Haarlem, Corrie and her father saw a sign in a store window: "Jews Will Not Be Served." Soon similar signs appeared at the entrances to theaters, restaurants, and parks. And

before long, all Jewish people were required to wear a yellow star pinned to their clothing. They could not hide, for on the star was written *Jood* (the Dutch word for "Jew"). And then Jewish-owned shops were forced to close, and Jewish families started to mysteriously disappear. On another daily walk, Corrie and her father saw men, women, and children—all wearing the yellow star—being loaded into the back of military trucks. Soldiers stood guard around them. The trucks roared out of Haarlem, and Corrie never saw those families again.

Corrie longed to help her Jewish neighbors. All her life, her family had prayed for the Jews, but she wanted to do more. Her brother Willem, now a pastor in the Dutch Reformed Church, was helping Jews find places to hide on farms in the countryside. And in November of 1941 Corrie saw her opportunity.

It was a cold autumn morning when she watched a group of Gestapo march down her street. They stopped directly across from the Beje and entered a Jewish-owned shop. The soldiers forced Mr. Weil, the shop-owner, out into the brick-paved street. Then they ransacked his shop and apartment. The old man shivered as soldiers heaved clothes and coats out the windows. When no one was looking, Corrie and Betsie ran across the street and brought Mr. Weil into the Beje.

As they sat around the dining room table, the Ten Booms and their neighbor discussed what could be done. They all agreed that Mr. Weil couldn't return home. It was too dangerous. Instead, he would need to find a safe place to live—to hide! And now Corrie knew what to do. She would ask her brother to help.

Determined to help their neighbor, Corrie boarded the train for Willem's town. When Corrie arrived after a three-hour train ride, she met with her twenty-one-year-old nephew, Christiaan (who everyone called Kik). She told Kik all about the situation. Without hesitation, he said, "Tell Mr. Weil to be ready as soon as it's dark."

That night right before the 9 p.m. curfew, Kik arrived at the Beje's side alley door. Minutes later he and Mr. Weil stepped out into the blackened, empty streets. And almost like a magic trick, they disappeared into the night. How were her brother and nephew able to help people escape? Were they working with others?

A few weeks later Corrie saw her nephew and asked about Mr. Weil. Kik smiled, "If you're going to work with the Underground, Aunt Corrie, you must learn not to ask questions."

Corrie had heard about the Dutch Underground movement, who secretly undermined the Nazis. Corrie wondered, *Was Kik collaborating with this illegal, resistance group? Was Willem?* And if she had helped Mr. Weil hide from the Gestapo, was *she* now part of the Underground too?

She hoped so.

In all the darkness of the Nazi invasion, Corrie now saw a glimmer of hope. A way to help the people that she had prayed for all her life. She had helped Mr. Weil, but again she wanted to do more.

Ration Cards

May–June 1942

BY MAY 1942, conditions were getting worse. Like
the turning of a screw, Nazi restrictions grew tighter
and tighter. The Jews could be arrested for no reason,
and curfew was now 8 p.m. Still Corrie wanted to
help. She kept praying, "Lord Jesus, I offer myself
for your people. In any way. Any place. Any time."

Although the freezing Dutch winter had warmed into spring, food became scarce, and the government made everyone use ration cards. Corrie could buy the food listed on her card, but when she used up the

— Tulips —

Did you know that Holland is famous for its bright, colorful tulips? However tulips aren't even originally from Holland! Tulips are actually from Asia and were brought to the Netherlands during the 1500s. At first tulips in Holland were rare and very special. Some people used tulip bulbs as if they were money. And people who had tulips in their gardens were in danger of thieves stealing their flowers. But before long growing tulips in gardens became less risky, and the love for this eye-catching flower spread across the Netherlands. Every year many Dutch towns hold tulip festivals and welcome millions of visitors who travel to see the colorful tulip gardens.

coupons for a certain item, that item was unavailable for the rest of the month. So when Dutch families ran out of potatoes, some of them ate tulip bulbs instead. Even tea and coffee were hard to find. Betsie used the same tea leaves repeatedly and happily served weak tea to anyone who came to the Beje, even though it was more like colored water.

But even as the food supply shriveled, the answer to Corrie's prayer began to sprout. One warm spring evening shortly before curfew, someone knocked on the alleyway door on the side of the Beje. Who could this be? The police station was only a block away. Corrie quickly made her way from the dining room down the short flight of steps to the door. She looked out the window. A woman she didn't recognize was wearing winter clothes and carrying a suitcase.

Corrie opened the door. In a shaking, high-pitched voice, the stranger introduced herself, "Can I come in? . . . My name is Kleermaker. I'm a Jew."

Corrie immediately took the lady up to the dining room. Papa pulled out a chair for her, and Betsie made her a cup of tea. Mrs. Kleermaker explained that her son was hiding from the authorities and her husband had been arrested. She had heard that the Ten Booms could be trusted, so she had come for help. Papa replied, "In this household, . . . God's people are always welcome." And Betsie added, "We have four empty beds upstairs. . . . Your problem will be choosing which one to sleep in!"

Two evenings later, more people, an old man and woman, knocked on the alleyway door. They too held suitcases. The Ten Booms welcomed this Jewish couple as well. Unfortunately while the empty bedrooms were filling up, the kitchen pantry was being emptied. Not only did the Ten Booms need to keep their visitors safe, they also had to keep them fed. And that would be almost as difficult! Ration cards were not available to Jewish people.

Not knowing what to do as her home filled up with fugitives and as the pantry ran out of supplies, Corrie again took the train to visit Willem. She asked him for food ration cards. But this was an almost impossible request. Ration cards were difficult to find and could not be faked.

"Willem, if people need ration cards and there aren't any counterfeit ones, what do they do?"

"Ration cards? . . . You steal them."

Corrie could not believe that her brother (a pastor!) was suggesting to steal the cards. But she couldn't let the three guests staying in the Beje starve. Could Willem steal the cards?

"No, Corrie! I'm watched! . . . Every move I make is watched! . . . It will be far better for you to develop your own sources."

For three hours on the train ride home, Corrie thought about Willem's words and how to feed three people. But when she entered the Beje, she found yet another couple who had come for help. Now she had five extra people to feed!

Then Corrie remembered Fred Koornstra. He had been their meterman. (A meterman went from house to house reading the dial, or "meter," that showed how much electricity or gas a family had used. This determined how much the family's bill would be each month.) But now Fred worked for the Food Office. And he would have access to ration cards! That evening, Corrie rode her bike over the brick streets to Fred's house. The rubber tires of her bicycle had worn out, and there were no replacement tires. So she bumped and scraped along on the metal rims.

When Corrie knocked on Fred's door, she prayed, *Lord, . . . if it is not safe to confide in Fred, stop this conversation before it is too late.* The door opened, and he invited her in. Corrie told Fred that she had visitors at the Beje. Jewish visitors. She carefully watched Fred's face. How would he respond to her secret? He didn't react. He just listened.

"Fred, is there any way you can give out extra cards? More than you report?"

"None at all, Corrie. Those cards have to be accounted for a dozen ways. They're checked and double-checked. . . . Unless—"

Unless?—What was Fred going to say about the cards?

— What Were Ration Cards? —

Because of the war, the Netherlands could not get shipments of specific items (imports) from other countries. And the German government took most Dutch-grown food and sent it back to Germany. This caused a shortage of food and household goods. To help balance or "ration" the limited resources available to Dutch citizens, the government issued ration coupons. Each person had a specific number of coupons to exchange for food or other goods. The Nazi government gave ration cards to the Dutch people, but not to the Jewish people. The Jews living throughout Holland had to find food on their own.

"Unless there should be a hold-up. . . . If it happened at noon . . . when just the record clerk and I were there . . . and if they found us tied and gagged. . . . And I know just the man who might do it! Do you remember the—"

Corrie held up her hand to stop him. She did not want to know any more details about this staged robbery! Fred nodded and asked her how many cards she would need. She needed five extra ration cards. But instead of saying, "Five," she said, "One hundred!"

A week later someone knocked on the Beje's side door. Instead of a having a suitcase, this person had black eyes and a swollen lip. It was Fred. (His friend who staged the robbery had done a convincing job!)

Fred handed Corrie a brown envelope. And inside were a hundred ration cards! To keep the cards safe, Corrie hid them with the radio inside the staircase. Before he left, Fred promised to figure out more ways to steal cards and bring them to Corrie. He would dress in his old meterman uniform and visit the Beje in disguise.

Ever since Corrie had helped Mr. Weil escape that winter, she had prayed that God would use her in any way and at any time. And just like the Dutch tulips were in beautiful bloom that spring, Corrie's

— Bicycles in Holland —

Since the late 1800s, bicycles have been an import-ant part of the Dutch culture. It wasn't uncommon to see firefighters and delivery drivers using spe-cialty bikes. When Corrie was thirty years old, there were around two million bikes in the Netherlands. And only about thirty thousand cars. That means that for every one car on the street, there were about sixty-seven bikes!

By the time World War II started, the Netherlands had over four million bicycles. But during the war, the Nazis took almost half of all those bikes. They sent the bicycles to Germany for their soldiers to ride. And some bikes were dismantled, with metal and rubber being recycled to make parts for German weapons and supplies. The Dutch people who still owned bikes rode on the metal rims, without rubber tires (which were impossible to get anymore). And some people crafted wheels made of wood.

opportunities also began to unfold with every knock on the Beje's side door.

A few nights later brought another knock at the door. It was past curfew, and the streets were dark and quiet. Corrie cracked open the door. And to her surprise, Kik stood in the alley.

"Get your bicycle, Aunt Corrie, . . . and put on a sweater. I have some people I want you to meet."

Kik wrapped cloth around Corrie's bare bicycle wheels to muffle the noise of metal against the bricks. Then they pedaled off into the darkness. She didn't know where they were going. And she didn't know how this late-night ride would change everything for her, her family, and the people hiding at the Beje.

6

The Secret Room

Summer 1942

CORRIE AND KIK BIKED QUIETLY through the night-time air, along dark winding streets, and across the Leidsevaart (lied-seh-VART) Canal bridge. Their three-mile ride brought them to a large, beautiful home in the village of Aerdenhout. Kik carried their bikes up the steps and into the house. Dozens of bare-rimmed bicycles crammed the entry. It looked more like a bike shop than a grand hallway!

Large rooms branched off the hall, and each room brimmed with people talking in small groups. Corrie scanned the crowds. Did she know anyone? And who did Kik want her to meet? Across the room, she saw a familiar face—Herman Sluring. He was a prominent man in Haarlem and a friend of her father. Herman handed her a cup of coffee—*real* coffee! And as Corrie sipped and savored the dark, rich flavor, he introduced her to several people standing near her: Mr. Smit, Mrs. Smit, and another Mr. Smit. Corrie was puzzled. Kik informed her that everyone used the name Smit; that's what you did in the resistance movement.

Resistance movement? Corrie stopped sipping her coffee. She then realized Herman was talking again. He had introduced her to the group as "the head of an operation here in this city"! *What was he saying? How were two middle-aged ladies and their elderly father running an operation? And she wasn't the head of anything!*

When the introduction was over, several of the Smits offered to help her Underground work. They could supply her with forged signatures, fake

— Using Code —

The Ten Boom family had been without a telephone since the Nazis cut off telephone service in 1940. But resistance workers helped reinstall the family's phone. With a working phone, they could run their Underground operations more efficiently. But they still had to be careful. Someone might be listening to their calls. So they used coded messages.

When someone called the Beje, Corrie might ask, "Is this about a watch?"

And if a Jewish woman needed a place to hide, the caller might say, "We have a woman's watch here that needs repairing."

And Corrie might respond saying, "Send the watch over, and I'll see what we can do in our own shop."

identification papers, and cars with phony license plates. Then a small man approached. He'd been standing off in a corner. As she expected, he introduced himself as Mr. Smit. But what she didn't expect was that he knew about the Beje. "Your house needs a secret room, and I'd like to build it! This room would provide a hiding place for your guests if the police searched your house."

Mr. Smit warned her, "This is a danger for all, those you are helping as well as yourselves and those who work with you. With your permission I will pay you a visit in the coming week."

Just a few days later Mr. Smit came to the Beje. The house was a puzzling mishmash—the perfect place to create a hidden room. The three floors of the narrow original house did not align with the four floors of the small skinny house behind it. Who could tell where one house began and the other ended? Mr. Smit began to climb, round and round, up the wooden spiral staircase. As he reached each landing and saw the Beje's odd nature—two homes cobbled into one—

he couldn't help but smile. "What an improbably, unbelievable, unpredictable impossibility!"

Once Mr. Smit reached the top of the stairs, he entered Corrie's small room. "This is it!" The delight shone on his face behind his small goatee. "You want your hiding place as high as possible. . . . Gives you the best chance to reach it while the search is below."

Corrie's room was the perfect place, even though it was small: only 10 feet by 7 feet. Mr. Smit began moving furniture, measuring walls, and making plans. He would build a false wall where the book-shelves stood. It would be brick so, unlike a wooden wall, there would be no echo if someone knocked on it. The secret room would be long and narrow: 2 feet by 8 feet. (That's about as deep as two school lockers pushed together and about as wide as eight lockers lined up side by side.) It was just big enough for a few people to hide. Throughout the following week, Mr. Smit and his workmen carefully smuggled their tools and materials into the Beje. Briefcases hid bricks and newspapers covered building supplies.

By the end of the week, Corrie, Betsie, and their father admired the new wall. And yet it didn't look new. The craftsmen had carefully preserved the original trim and uneven paint, maintaining the look of

the 150-year-old house. Along the new wall stood the bookshelves and a linen cabinet. Behind the cabinet, hidden by its lower shelves, was a trap door. A small panel slid up to allow access to the secret narrow room. Corrie, Betsie, and Mr. Smit crawled through the trap door and experienced the size and feel of the hidden space.

Mr. Smit, who Corrie only later learned was an acclaimed architect, gave detailed instructions: food and water, as well as the guests' belongings, should always be left inside the hiding place. And Corrie should continue to live in her bedroom.

Mr. Smit admired the wall. "The Gestapo could search for a year. . . . They'll never find this one." Corrie hoped so. And soon the secrecy of the hidden room would be tested.

Jesus Is Victor

Autumn 1942–February 1944

THROUGH THE AUTUMN AND WINTER, Corrie's team of Underground resistance workers grew to over eighty members. They rescued Jewish orphans and transported them to safe homes. They distributed stolen ration cards. They gave temporary housing at the Beje to hundreds of people before smuggling them to the Dutch countryside where they could hide permanently. Corrie, Betsie, and their father called themselves "God's Underground."

In June 1943 the Ten Booms began hiding people permanently at the Beje. Eventually seven refugees lived

— Life While Hiding —

What was everyday life like in Nazi-occupied Holland? For some, life was dangerous. Each day brought new threats for specific groups during the war: Jewish people, Underground workers, and any young man able to work in German factories. These young Dutchmen became known as "underdivers" or "divers." Because in the same way that some fish will dive deep in the water to avoid a fisherman's net, these young men went deep into hiding to avoid being captured by the Nazis.

For others, life seemed more normal. The Ten Boom family worked for the Underground, but despite wartime limitations and many guests, full-time with Corrie's family. They found life at the Beje to be sweet, but they were always in danger. The police station sat just around the corner, only a block away.

Because the Gestapo might raid at any time, the guests could not unpack and settle into their new

they tried to carry on as if nothing extraordinary were happening. In the evenings, everyone in the Beje came together to sing and read plays and books aloud. Two of the permanent guests played piano and violin. And two other permanent guests taught the group Italian and Hebrew lessons. And every evening included prayer and Bible reading. When the government restricted the use of electricity, the Ten Booms used candles. But candles were not always available. So during those times, they placed Corrie's bicycle, which had a headlight, onto a raised stand. When someone pedaled, the bike light lit up a corner of the room. This pedal-powered light provided hours of delight during the dark nights.

rooms. Instead, they kept their belongings in the hiding place. So Corrie's small bedroom had a constant stream of people coming and going, getting their things. With all this activity, Corrie said that her room felt like a beehive!

To help bring some order to the beehive, one of the Beje's permanent guests, a young Dutchman named Leendart, installed an alarm notification system. He wired a buzzer at the top of the staircase and several hidden buttons across the house and shop. If the police were to come, someone could push a button to warn the refugees to hide.

Knowing that the Gestapo could raid the Beje at anytime, Corrie ran practice drills for the entire house—some during meals and some in the middle of the night. And she personally prepared as well. She packed a "prison bag"—with her Bible, extra clothes, medicine, and various other items. She was ready if the Gestapo came.

As the months passed, the Underground work grew more dangerous. The shop and the Beje began to buzz with an unusually large number of people coming and going. Would the neighbors become suspicious of so many people needing "watch repairs"? Like the risks and rewards of beekeeping, Corrie's family were taking risks. And Corrie wondered how long it might be before they'd get stung.

Mealtime was especially risky; the dining room faced the alleyway. Although the window was five steps above the street level, a mere café curtain shielded the large circle of guests from public view. One day in September 1943, Corrie glanced up at the window during a meal and saw a face peering over the top of the curtain that covered the bottom half of the window. To see over the curtain, he had to have been on a 10-foot ladder. Eusie, one of the Jewish refugees, saw him too and, thinking quickly, began to sing "Happy Birthday" to Corrie's father. Instantly, all seventeen people around the table joined the singing. But the face at the window had disappeared. Was the man just washing the windows? Or was he working with the police?

By February 28, 1944, it had been five months since they saw the man peering over the dining room curtain. Thankfully, nothing had come from it, and Corrie had never seen him again. On this morning, she

— Practicing for a Raid —

Corrie ran practice drills for everyone hiding at the Beje. These drills helped Corrie see how fast the guests could climb the stairs and crawl into the hiding place. She might press a button hidden under the dining room window. If everyone were at dinner, the guests would jump from their chairs carrying their dishes with them. Then Corrie, Betsie, and their father would rearrange the table setting and chairs to look like a small family meal. The first drill took four minutes. That was far too long! If the Gestapo had come, the Jews and divers would have been caught.

So over and over—during the day and the middle of the night—Corrie ran surprise drills. She woke up like most mornings with the sound of the permanent guests shuffling in and out of her room. They were all returning their nightclothes to the hiding place. Corrie was thankful for the slow, simple

pressed the button and the buzzer sounded. The Jews and divers sprang into action. If the drill happened at night, the guests also made sure to flip their mattresses. The Gestapo always checked to see if an empty bed were warm. (A warm bed meant that someone had been sleeping there recently.) Since the buzzer could ring during the day or night, the guests kept all of their belongings in the hiding place.

After many practices, the group got their time down to 70 seconds. It became a challenge to see if they could beat their earlier time. And after each drill, Corrie used her ration coupons to reward everyone with cream puffs from the local bakery.

morning because she was sick. She had a fever, was coughing, and had barely left her bed for two days.

Betsie brought her tea and let her know that a man in the shop had asked to speak with her. Although sick and exhausted, Corrie dressed and slowly made her way down the stairs. Once she reached the shop, she greeted the small man with the code: "Is it about a watch?"

"No, Miss Ten Boom, something far more serious!" He began his story, like so many she'd heard before. His wife had been arrested, and he needed 600 guilders (Dutch currency) to bribe the police.

Even through the drowsiness of her fever, Corrie noticed the man's eyes. As he talked, he never looked at her. Was something wrong? Feeling ill but still wanting to help, Corrie said, "Come back in half an hour. I'll have the money."

Corrie returned to the house and instructed one of the resistance workers to prepare the money. She trudged back upstairs, passing the sitting room where Willem and Nollie were holding their weekly prayer meeting. She returned to bed and fell asleep. But not for long. Suddenly the alarm buzzed wildly. And hushed voices rushed into her room. This was no drill. The Gestapo had come!

She jumped out of bed counting the bodies disappearing through the trap door. One, two, . . . five, six. *Six? Yes, that was the right number*, she thought. She remembered that Leendart was away on business for the resistance movement. Then seeing her briefcase full of illegal Underground documents, she threw in the case, closed the trap door, and slid into bed. Just as she lay back, the door flew open.

A large man in a blue suit barreled into the room. "So you're the ring leader! Tell me now, where are you hiding the Jews?"

Acting sleepy, Corrie crawled out of bed and put on her glasses. "I don't know what you're talking about." She put on her dress and sweater over her pajamas. She had rehearsed this moment dozens of times. But then she saw her prison bag. It sat right beside the trap door. If she picked it up, would she draw attention to the secret panel? Corrie later said, "It was the hardest thing I had ever done to turn and walk out of that room, leaving the bag behind."

The large man led Corrie down the stairs and into the shop. "Where are the Jews?" he demanded.

Even with her fever, Corrie remembered what she had practiced. She answered confidently, "There aren't any Jews here."

He slapped her across the face. "Where do you hide the ration cards?" He struck her again and again.

Corrie cried out, "Lord Jesus, . . . protect me!"

The man's hand stopped short of another hit. "If you say that name again, I'll kill you."

But the beating stopped, and he led Corrie back to the dining room. As she sat at the table with her father and sister, the Gestapo searched the entire house and shop. They found the radio, but they did *not* find the secret room.

The dining room became filled with people—the shop workers and the people from Willem and Nollie's prayer meeting. Betsie, Corrie, and their father exchanged glances, and Betsie silently directed their eyes to the wooden plaque beside the fireplace. Pink flowers decorated the white letters: "Jesus is Victor." Corrie looked at the plaque and thought, *It looks now as if the Gestapo were the conquerors. But they are not. I do not understand it all, but believing is not the same as understanding.*

When they had finished their search, the Gestapo marched the group out of the house and down the alley, and around the block toward the police station. Thirty-five people were arrested at the Beje during the raid that day. That evening, just like every evening of Corrie's life, her father gathered the group for Bible reading and prayer. Without a Bible to read from, her Father quoted Psalm 91:

> He who dwells in the shelter of the Most High
>   will abide in the shadow of the Almighty.
> I will say to the LORD, "My refuge and my fortress,
>   my God, in whom I trust."

Then, Casper ten Boom, their beloved papa, surrounded by his four children and dozens of friends,

prayed for the Lord's protection. Corrie could never have realized that after fifty-one years of nightly prayers with her father, this would be their last. The next day the prisoners filed out of the police station and boarded an awaiting green bus. Corrie was leaving all she had known—her home and her watchmaking career. But as the noisy engine rumbled down the cold, sunny streets of Haarlem, Corrie felt peace in her heart.

Though Corrie had protected hundreds of other people, she was now a prisoner. Though the German Gestapo had destroyed their resistance work, she knew Jesus was still the victor. No matter what happened, Jesus was her refuge. Even through dark days, Jesus would be her hiding place.

Light in the Darkness

February–June 1944

ON FEBRUARY 29, 1944, prison vehicles rolled through the tall iron gates of Scheveningen prison. Inside the thick brick walls, a four-story building towered over several low buildings scattered within the sprawling complex. This Dutch federal prison was controlled by the Nazi government. The guards hustled the new prisoners into one of the low-roofed buildings. In a long line, the prisoners moved from one desk to the next. Corrie, her family, and the others handed over their belongings—watches, rings, wallets. Then came an interrogation that lasted for hours.

Finally, the guards marched the prisoners into a large room. A guard shouted, "Noses to the wall!" Corrie didn't know how long she stood examining the cracks and marks in the rough wall in front of her. Finally, a door opened and a female guard appeared. She yelled, "Women prisoners follow me."

Corrie looked back and saw her Papa. "Father! . . . God be with you!"

His blue eyes shone behind his glasses as he turned his face. "And with you, my daughters."

His words echoed in her ears, as the guard marched Corrie and her sisters down a long hallway lined with solid cell doors. The guard stopped in front of a narrow cell, six paces long and two paces wide. A single light bulb hung from the ceiling. And four winter coats and hats hung on the hooks on the rough brick wall.

Four women already occupied this cell. One lay on a low bed and three sat on mattresses on the floor. Corrie stepped inside. The guard barked, "Give this one the cot. . . . She's sick," and she slammed the heavy door. Even on a stale straw mattress, Corrie was glad to lie down. But with the dust in the air, her coughing intensified, and her body ached.

For two weeks, Corrie suffered with sickness in that cramped, windowless cell. Until, finally, the guards let her visit a local doctor's office. As Corrie waited, a nurse quietly asked, "Is there any way I can help?"

Corrie blinked with surprise. "Yes. Oh yes! A Bible! . . . A toothbrush! And soap!"

When the doctor came in, he listened to Corrie's cough and took her temperature. He diagnosed her as having a painful disease of the lungs with a long name: tuberculous pleural effusion. It hurt to cough, laugh, or even take a breath.

Back in the waiting room, the nurse pressed a small object into Corrie's hand. Corrie slipped it into her pocket. Back in her cell, she opened the paper-wrapped package. It felt like Christmas morning. Inside the package was soap and four small booklets: the Gospels—Matthew, Mark, Luke, and John! But having God's word in a Nazi prison could bring beatings or even death. So Corrie carefully concealed the booklets in her coat pocket.

Despite her doctor visit, Corrie's fever continued, and her excruciating cough persisted. The doctor feared that she would infect other prisoners. So two nights later, a guard led Corrie to a new cell. It was the same as the last one, except high up the far wall was a window, and there were no cellmates. This was solitary confinement.

The next three months were some of the most difficult and dark times in Corrie's life. Her straw mattress reeked of disease from a previous sick prisoner. And the cold wind battered the outside wall. Still dressed in her pajamas beneath her dress, she wrapped her coat around her. She coughed up blood, and her chest ached.

All the prisoners in Scheveningen endured difficulties. Food was scarce. No one could sing or talk
from cell to cell. Some endured beatings. And some
were killed. And almost all endured questioning by
German officers. These interrogations could last for
hours. *Did you hide Jews? Who do you know in the Dutch
Underground?*

For weeks Corrie wondered about her family.
And about the Beje—what had happened to the six
people in the hiding place? And she longed for the
items left behind in her prison bag—*a fresh blouse,
a whole bottle of aspirin, toothpaste with a peppermint
taste*. And through all her darkness, Corrie poured
out her heart to God. Day after day, she would pray,
"O Savior, you are with me. Help me; hold me fast
and comfort me."

As the cold winter turned to spring, Corrie grew
stronger and recovered from the tuberculosis.
Streams of warm sunlight began to fill her cell. She
watched the clouds float by and the stars shine at
night. And when the wind blew just right, she could

hear the waves crashing on the nearby shore. She read the four Gospel booklets again and again, remembering once more the life, suffering, and death of Jesus. And as she gained strength and read, the light dawned in her heart, and her thoughts began to clear: *Was it possible that the war, this prison cell, and being alone were not an accident?*

As warmer weather found its way into Corrie's cell, so too did letters and packages from home. And if the guards allowed it, she had paper and pen to write back. Corrie learned that almost everyone who had been arrested at the Beje had been released. Only she and Betsie were still in prison. But no one had heard from her father or what had happened to the Jews they had been hiding.

One day, Corrie received a package from Nollie. She carefully opened it, and inside, discovered wonders: cookies, a needle and thread, a red towel, and her sister's own blue sweater. Corrie smiled. Vivid colors in such a drab cell were like a vibrant rainbow after a storm. But then Corrie noticed something odd about the front of the box. The writing on the package was slanting up toward the corner. So she slowly peeled back the stamp. A secret message lay hidden underneath! Corrie sobbed. Through her tears she read the tiny words that held such big meaning, "All the watches in your closet are safe." The people in the hiding place had escaped!

Despite having little food, rarely having access to a shower or clean clothes, and being alone with no one to talk to for months, Corrie tried to find joy in her circumstances. On April 11, Corrie wrote in a letter, "Sometimes it may be dark, but the Savior provides his light, and how wonderful that is." And she also learned to enjoy some tiny new cellmates: ants! She watched them come and go. And she fed them crumbs from her own meals. Then on April 15, 1944, she celebrated her fifty-second birthday.

Two weeks later, the opening line in a letter from Nollie caused her to stop. "Corrie, can you be very brave?"

No! she thought. *No, I couldn't be brave!* Corrie continued reading—their father had died only ten days after being arrested. Corrie couldn't move. There was no one to cry with, talk to, or to hug. Then she heard a guard in the hallway and called out to her.

"What's the matter?" the guard snapped.

Corrie began, "This letter just came. . . . It says that my father—it says my father has died."

"Whatever happens, . . . you brought it on yourself by breaking the laws!" The guard's footsteps echoed in the hall as she marched away.

Corrie sat on her cot. "Dear Jesus, . . . how foolish of me to have called for human help when You are here." Despite her deep sorrow at losing her dear father, Corrie wrote, "How good the Savior is to me! He not only helps carry my burden; he carries me also."

At times, guards interrogated prisoners violently, for hours or days. And after months of solitary confinement, the day came for Corrie to face an interrogator. Yet when she entered the room, the guard

was not alone. In front of her stood Betsie, Willem, and Nollie. After three months, her siblings were together again, even if for just a few minutes. They had been summoned to read their father's will. And when the guard was turned, Nollie slipped Corrie a tiny stringed bag with a Bible inside. Corrie quickly slid the strings around her neck and let the bag hang under her dress.

When Corrie later returned to her cell, somehow it seemed brighter than before. God's word flooded her heart and mind with the warmth of his love and light. Corrie later remembered, "I talked with my Savior. Never before had fellowship with him been so close. It was a joy I hoped would continue unchanged. I was a prisoner—and yet . . . how free!"

And Corrie shone this light for others. She began leaving pages from her four Gospel booklets in the bathhouse or slid them through cracks in the walls. This was good news for everyone.

And other news began to reach the prison. The prisoners heard whispers of an impending attack against Germany. And to Corrie's surprise, suddenly on June 6, 1944, the guards rushed all the prisoners to a nearby train station.

That same day, 350 miles to the south, over one hundred thousand American and British soldiers landed on the beaches of Normandy, France. The Allied invasion would eventually bring liberation to Nazi-occupied Europe. Victory was dawning, but for Corrie and Betsie, their darkest days were still ahead.

Fear and Forgiveness

June–September 1944

HUNDREDS OF PRISONERS stood at attention waiting for the train to take them away—not to freedom,
but to their next prison.

Corrie scanned the rows of prisoners, looking for
her sister, Betsie. Finally, as the sun was setting in
the west, she saw her. So as the train approached,

Corrie wormed and shoved through the crowd to grab Betsie's hand. Through their tears of joy, they climbed the train steps. They were together for the first time in four months, aside from the few minutes during the reading of their father's will. *But where were they headed now?*

The train traveled 60 miles southeast to the Dutch town of Vught, farther from home and closer to Germany. Unlike Scheveningen—a Dutch federal prison—Vught Prison was a concentration camp built by the Nazis specifically for Jews and political prisoners. These prison camps (also called labor camps) were designed to hold large numbers of prisoners who performed hard labor and endured awful living conditions.

The Vught guards distributed the women's prison uniforms: blue overalls with a red stripe on the side, blue polka dot headscarves, and wooden shoes. Corrie and Betsie entered Barrack 23B. Bunkbeds lined every wall. Over 150 other women lived inside this one barrack. Corrie and Betsie shared their bed with another woman.

Even the hardness of life in the prison camp became routine. Every day they woke up at 5 a.m. and had bread and coffee for breakfast. Roll call was at 6 a.m. Each morning the guards counted the rows of prisoners as they stood at attention. If a prisoner were late or had broken a rule, the whole group would be punished with a 4 a.m. roll call the next day. The 12-hour workday lasted until 6:30 p.m., except on Sundays when work finished at 12:30 p.m. In the evening, the prisoners stood for another roll call and then ate a meager dinner. Bedtime was 9 p.m. Vught Prison was a relief from the extreme isolation of Scheveningen. But the sisters were still in prison, and they were never out of danger.

Every prisoner at Vught was required to work. Betsie, at fifty-eight years old, was weak and suffered from a severe vitamin B12 deficiency. The prison officials gave her an easy job—sewing clothes for German soldiers. And Corrie worked at the makeshift Philips "Factory" located in Barrack 35. The Nazis had taken control of this Dutch electronics company and forced prisoners to make radio parts for German aircraft.

Corrie's first job was simply sorting small glass cylinders. But once the foreman, who was a fellow prisoner, learned that she was a watchmaker, he gave her more skilled work. She became the last step of the assembly line; her job was to inspect the radios. One day her foreman came by her workbench and exclaimed, "Dear watch lady! Can you not remember for whom you are working? These radios are for their fighter planes!" He then pulled loose some of the radio wires and told her to reattach them the wrong way!

The harsh difficulties of every day's routine was nothing compared to the brutal surprises that sometimes awaited them. During a long roll call, a pregnant prisoner fell and hit her head. The guards did not stop calling the roll or move to help her. The prisoners also regularly heard gunshots echoing across the camp. And one day Corrie saw male prisoners with shaved heads and striped uniforms digging ditches on their side of the camp. *Were they digging graves?* Corrie and Betsie never knew when their names would be called to join the groups marching to the far side of the camp. Many other women had marched away and had never come back.

The months of brutal prison life caused Corrie's hair to turn from brown to gray. And in July, a guard caught her talking to a non-prisoner working in the Philips workroom. This was forbidden! Corrie was summoned to the camp office. Would she be beaten? Tortured? Killed? The officer made a note in Corrie's file but only gave her a warning. In a letter to Nollie on August 13, Corrie wrote that she was "learning to put the worst into the hands of the Savior."

Despite their living conditions, long workdays, and the danger, Corrie and Betsie saw opportunities to point other prisoners to Jesus. In the evenings they held a prayer meeting around their bunkbed. And on Sunday afternoons, Corrie and several others held a worship service on the grass near the barracks. Corrie later recalled: "Never before had I prayed as now. There was so much sorrow among these prisoners,

. . . above whose heads still hung so dire a threat. And I spoke to one who understood, who knew us and loved us. On him I cast all our burdens."

In the evenings the sisters shared the news of their day at work. And one evening, Betsie had learned difficult news. She had heard why the Gestapo had arrested their family: they had been betrayed by the man who came to the watch shop the day of their arrest. His name was Jan Vogel; he was a Dutchman

who worked with the Nazis. Because of his treachery, Corrie had been ripped from her home, her health had been damaged, her family broken, and her father killed.

Corrie grew angry. She later said, "Flames of fire seemed to leap . . . in my heart. I thought of Father's final hours. . . . And I knew that if Jan Vogel stood in front of me now, I could kill him." For days, Corrie couldn't sleep. She closed her eyes. But like a movie

replaying in her mind, she couldn't stop reliving her conversation in the watch shop with Vogel.

During the day at her workbench all she could talk about was this horrible man. Yet Betsie hardly said a word about him. Finally, Corrie could take her big sister's silence no longer. Later that week, crammed in their bunkbed, Corrie blurted out, "Betsie, don't you feel anything about Jan Vogel? Doesn't it bother you?"

"Oh yes, Corrie! Terribly!" Betsie turned to look her sister in the eye. "I've felt for him ever since I knew—and pray for him whenever his name comes into my mind. How dreadfully he must be suffering!"

How could Vogel be suffering!? He was the guilty one! He had betrayed her family. Then Corrie thought, *But haven't I also been guilty of hatred?* She had sinned too. She had killed him with her heart and with her words. Then Corrie quietly prayed, "Lord Jesus, . . . I forgive Jan Vogel as I pray that you will forgive me. I have done him great damage. Bless him now, and his family." And that night, Corrie finally slept.

— The Weaver —

How did Corrie make sense of all the suffering and evil she had witnessed? As she thought about the horrors of prison, she often said her life was like an embroidered tapestry. The bottom side looks jumbled and snarled. But when you see the top side, it's a beautiful picture. Corrie wrote, "Although the threads of my life have often seemed knotted, I know, by faith, that on the other side of the embroidery there is a Crown."

Corrie loved to quote the poem "The Weaver" written by Grant Colfax Tullar. The poem tells the story of God being the great weaver:

Oft' times He weaveth sorrow;
And I in foolish pride
Forget He sees the upper
And I the underside.

In September rumors reached them that the Allied Forces were advancing and had crossed the Dutch border. But spreading rumors could get a prisoner killed. Across the camp, the guards were nervous and became more vicious. On the women's side of the prison, the guards beat some of the sick prisoners for being late to roll call. And on the men's side, the loudspeaker echoed the voice of a guard reading a long list of names—husbands, sons, and fathers. When the microphone went silent, the gunfire began. Hundreds of Dutchmen died that day.

That night, Corrie pulled her thin cloth blanket up to her chin. She thought about all she had endured. What was God doing? What was God's plan for her life? In her mind, it was like a thick colorful fabric with woven threads creating an elaborate and lovely picture. But right now, she could only see the twisted threads on the bottom side of the cloth. She thought, *Everything looks like a confused piece of embroidery work, meaningless and ugly. But that is the underside. Someday we shall see the right side and shall be amazed and thankful.*

The next day the Nazis abandoned Vught prison and packed the remaining prisoners into a freight train. The eighty women crammed in Corrie and Betsie's boxcar could barely move. Eventually, they managed a seating arrangement where each person sat with her legs circling the woman in front of her. Corrie said that it looked like they were sitting on a sled. For four days, the prisoners traveled with no restroom, and almost no food, water, or fresh air.

Corrie's life seemed to be nothing but a tangle of knots and jumbled thread—betrayal, prison, and loss. But God was teaching her how to forgive. And she was becoming even more confident that God doesn't make mistakes. Even if she couldn't see it yet, he was weaving a beautiful picture.

But the threads of Corrie's story would only grow more tangled. She and Betsie were headed out of Holland, deep into Germany: to Ravensbrück.

10

Ravensbrück

September–December 1944

CORRIE AND BETSIE CRAWLED out of the boxcar. They lugged dirty pillowcases that held their few possessions: toothbrushes, needle and thread, a bottle of medicine, and blankets. Ahead of the sisters stood the women-only prison: tall concrete walls, electrified fences, and guard towers. Rows and rows of gray buildings stretched from one side of the camp to the other. Ravensbrück was like a completely colorless city.

The guards marched the prisoners into a large one-story building. Then came the orders: "Drop all your belongings and clothes in this pile, then line up for the shower. After the shower, get your prison dress and shoes. Move along!"

Several male prison guards stood watch over the line of terrified women. One large guard—with thinning hair, blue-gray eyes, and taunting smile— laughed at the cowering prisoners.

Corrie stood beside her sister in the long line. *What could she do about her Bible that hung secretly from her neck? And what about her blue sweater from Nollie? Betsie was wearing it now and would need it to stay warm this winter.* Corrie dropped her pillowcase into the mounding pile, but she didn't take off her overalls. She had an idea!

Getting out of line, she and Betsie moved to the front and asked to use the restroom. The guard looked at the shower room. One group of women had just finished showering and were now in the changing room, putting on prison dresses, each one marked with an X on the front and back. The guard pointed toward the empty shower room, "Use the drain holes."

Alone in the shower room, the sisters quickly removed the blue sweater and the string bag that held the Bible. Before the next group came into the shower room, Corrie hid both items behind a stack of mildewing benches in a corner of the room, away from the showerheads. The sisters returned to the line, removed their overalls, and were soon ushered back into the shower room. Corrie showered and put on the thin prison dress. Then she quickly returned to the corner of the shower room to retrieve her secret stash and hide them all under her dress. The stringed bag holding the Bible hung between her shoulder blades.

As the prisoners filed out of the dressing room, the guards patted down each woman. They caught one woman smuggling a wool vest. Corrie prayed, *Lord, cause your angels to surround me. . . . Don't let the guards see me.* The guards searched the lady before Corrie. But when it was Corrie's turn, no guard touched her or even talked to her. Instead, they searched Betsie, the next person in line behind Corrie. Later Corrie said, "It was as though I was blocked out of their sight."

Although Corrie and Betsie only possessed a few smuggled items, they felt "rich in the care of him who was God even of Ravensbrück." Their new home, Barrack 28, contained a workroom and a bunkroom packed nearly wall to wall with rows of three-tiered bunkbeds. The room was built to hold four hundred women, but the sisters shared this space with 1,400 women. Seven women shared each bed. Corrie said that they slept like spoons in a silverware drawer. But more than just women filled the room. There were also fleas! The old straw mattresses crawled with the tiny bugs. Feeling bite after bite on her legs, Corrie scrambled out of the bunk. "Betsie, how can we live in such a place!?" Betsie reminded her little sister of the Bible verse they had read that morning: "Give thanks in all things." But Corrie wasn't so sure she could be thankful for fleas!

Life at Ravensbrück was intense, terrifying, and cruel. Between 1939 and 1945, over ninety thousand women died at Ravensbrück—from beatings, shootings, "medical" experiments, disease, lack of food, and exhaustion. The guards treated the women like animals, yet few were as cruel as the large guard with blue-gray eyes who had laughed at them when they arrived. He seemed to delight in the misery of the women. He made them suffer.

The daily demands of life at Ravensbrück were severe enough. Each day, the morning whistle sounded at 4 a.m., and roll call was at 4:30 a.m. Breakfast was bread and coffee. Lunch was a boiled potato and watery soup. And dinner was a single ladle of turnip soup. And for eleven hours a day, Corrie and Betsie labored, hauling heavy metal plates or shoveling dirt.

Yet each evening, the sisters held a worship service behind a row of bunkbeds. Prisoners from France,

Poland, Belgium, and Austria came together to read the Bible. Eventually their group grew so large that they started a second service. But even as the group grew, the prison guards never came into the bunkroom.

By November, cold and constant rains drenched the camp. The prisoners were now as thin as skeletons. They stood in roll call for hours, icy water puddling over their ankles. Plunging temperatures and bitter wind bit through their dresses. The thin prison-issued coats did little to block the freezing wind. So Corrie and Betsie stuffed smuggled newspapers under their clothes for added warmth.

On their job one day, Betsie was too weak to lift her shovel. A young female guard struck Betsie across the face and neck with a small leather whip. Impulsively Corrie grabbed her shovel and ran at the guard. But Betsie raised her hand to stop her. "Corrie! . . . Corrie, keep working." Corrie could see the blood on her sister's neck. Betsie pleaded with her, "Don't look at it, Corrie. Look at Jesus only."

A few days later Betsie went to the camp hospital. She had a 104-degree fever. After three days, she returned to the barrack. She still had a fever, so miraculously she and Corrie were able to begin a new job: knitting socks for German soldiers.

The knitting work crew met in the sisters' own barrack. As they knitted, Betsie and Corrie told their coworkers about Jesus. The prison guards rarely patrolled the workroom, and they never entered the bunkroom. Finally, Corrie found out why: It was the fleas! The guards knew the room was infested with fleas, so they kept their distance. Those little pests, that she hated so deeply, had given Corrie the freedom to sing hymns, pray, and host worship services. Corrie gave thanks to God for the fleas. She later said, "In the sanctuary of God's fleas, Betsie and I ministered the word of God to all in the room."

But despite her easier working conditions, Betsie only grew weaker. She began coughing up blood and could barely move her arms and legs. At night, lying in their crowded bunk Corrie held her frail big sister. Betsie talked about her dreams for life after prison. She envisioned opening a home in Holland where people affected by the war—both prisoner and prison guard—could heal emotionally. Betsie explained, "It's such a beautiful house, Corrie! The floors are all inlaid wood. . . . And gardens! . . . It will do them such good, Corrie, to care for flowers!"

Betsie explained that they wouldn't just help the Dutch people. One day they would open a facility to help German people too. It would be a former concentration camp. But there wouldn't be barbed wire or walls. Instead, flowers would fill window boxes. "The barracks are gray, Corrie, but we'll paint them green! Bright, light green, like springtime." Corrie leaned over her sister to hear her faint words: "We must tell them that there is no pit so deep that God is not deeper still. They will listen to us, Corrie, because we have been here."

A few days later, on December 16, 1944, Betsie died. She was fifty-nine years old. Corrie was alone again. But in this darkness, Corrie recalled that "God's presence was even more real. Even though I was looking into the valley of the shadow of death, I was not afraid. It is here that Jesus comes the closest, taking our hand and leading us through."

Three days after Betsie's death, the dreaded morning whistle blew as usual. And once more Corrie crawled out into the bitter cold and took her place in line, awaiting roll call. Her feet and hands were numb with cold. Her heart was numb with grief. Suddenly she snapped to attention. The loudspeaker was echoing her name: "Ten Boom, Cornelia." Why? Had the guards found the Bible? Was the guard with the blue-gray eyes waiting for her? Would she be tortured? Killed?

As more names were announced, Corrie silently prayed. A small group of women huddled together uncertain why they had been called, while rows and rows of other prisoners marched off to work. For three hours Corrie and the other women stood, waiting and wondering.

Then finally a female guard motioned for Corrie to follow her into a building. Inside, an official sat behind a large desk covered in papers. "Ten Boom, Cornelia," he called out. Corrie approached. The official stamped a paper and held it out to her. A guard standing nearby pointed her out into the hallway, and Corrie looked at the paper. "Certificate of Discharge." She could go home!

One moment she was imprisoned, and the next, she was free. "I still do not understand all the details of my release from Ravensbrück," Corrie later wrote. "All I know is, it was a miracle of God."

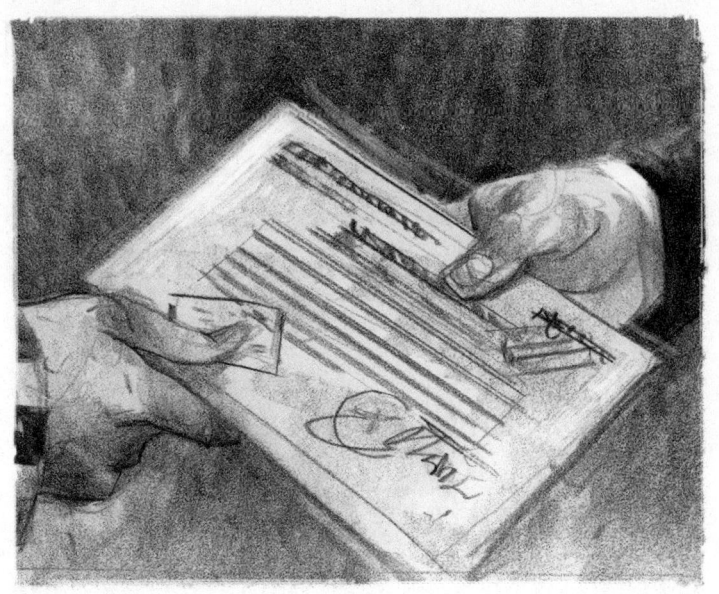

Home

1945–1959

CORRIE LOOKED OUT THE WINDOW as her train crossed the border. Though her body was worn down, joy bubbled in her heart. She was finally back in Holland, but the war was not over. German soldiers patrolled the towns, and travel was still restricted. The train went as far as the border town of Groningen.

Corrie hadn't eaten for days. She was hungry, weak, and dirty. She staggered to a Christian hospital a few blocks from the train station. Now *she* was the one knocking on a door looking for help. The nurses welcomed her in and brought her potatoes, brussels sprouts, meat and gravy, and for dessert, pudding with currant juice, and an apple. One of the nurses remarked that she had never seen someone eat "so intensely!" After Corrie ate her fill of the delicious Dutch foods, she took a hot bath. The first she had enjoyed in ten months. Every time a nurse knocked on the bathroom door, Corrie called out, "Five more minutes!" Finally, she crawled into a soft bed and slept all night on cool, clean sheets. She stayed at the hospital for ten days.

With the help of the Dutch Underground, Corrie returned to Haarlem—and to the Beje. Alone in the empty house, she climbed the stairs to the sitting room. The portrait of her father hung on the wall. His favorite chair sat vacant beside the fireplace. The dining room hosted no guests. But the memories replayed in her mind—the Jews seeking refuge, her Papa leading evening prayers, Betsie making tea, the wooden sign on the wall reminding the room: "Jesus is Victor."

Corrie was back in her beloved house, but, somehow, it no longer felt like home. She resumed her work in the watch shop as well. But she wanted to do more.

She wanted to do good, to truly help her hurting countrymen. The Nazis still controlled Holland, but their powerful grip was loosening. Corrie began to feel more freedom to tell her friends about her time in prison. At a small public meeting she explained her desire to open a home where people could heal from the emotional pain of prison and war. After the meeting, a well-dressed lady approached her. She said that her family owned a large home, called Schapenduinen House (SHOP-en-down-en), in the town of Bloemendaal, only four miles from Haarlem. She wanted to offer it as the place that Corrie mentioned—a place of healing for her broken, hurting countrymen.

A few weeks later, Corrie stood outside the sprawling fifty-six-room mansion. The well-dressed Mrs. Bierens de Haan began, "We've let the gardens go. . . . Don't you think released prisoners might find therapy in growing things?"

Corrie could hardly speak as she looked up at the grand house. She remembered Betsie's dreams for the future. Corrie asked, "Are there inlaid wood floors inside?"

"You've been here then?"

"No, . . . I heard about it from—" Corrie wasn't sure what to say.

Mrs. Bierens de Haan added, "From someone who's been here?"

Corrie smiled. "Yes, . . . from someone who's been here."

A month later, on May 5, 1945, the German forces in Holland surrendered. And three days later, the Canadian military liberated Haarlem. For Corrie the war was over!

In June, the mansion in Bloemendaal opened its doors to over a hundred people. Some of them had spent the war in prison. Others had hidden in attics or cellars. Many harbored anger and bitterness toward the Nazis, especially the Dutch Nazis who had betrayed their own country.

As Corrie saw healing come to so many men and women, she noticed a pattern: people who forgave

their enemies were able to heal and rebuild their lives; but people who remained bitter and hated their enemies were not able to heal or truly be free. Corrie later said, "Forgiveness is the key that unlocks the door of resentment and the handcuffs of hatred. It is a power that breaks the chains of bitterness."

— In Her Own Words —

On June 19, 1945, Corrie sent a letter to Jan Vogel, the man who had betrayed her family. He was on death row for his crimes against Holland. She wrote:

Dear Sir,

I heard that most probably you are the one who betrayed me. . . . The harm you planned was turned into good for me by God. I came nearer to him. . . .

I have forgiven you everything. God will also forgive you everything if you ask him. He loves you, and he himself sent his Son to earth to

That summer, Corrie invited several Dutch citizens who had been former Nazis to stay at the mansion in Bloemendaal, as well. These traitors were hated by their countrymen and needed healing. But fights broke out among the residents. So Corrie opened her beloved Beje as a separate rehabilitation home for the traitors.

reconcile your sins, which means to suffer the punishment for you and me. You on your part have to give an answer to this. If he says, "Come unto me; give me your heart," then your answer must be, "Yes, Lord, I come; make me your child." If it is difficult for you to pray, then ask if God will give you his Spirit, who works the faith in your heart. Never doubt the Lord Jesus's love. He is standing with his arms spread out to receive you.

I hope that the path that you will now take may work for your eternal salvation.

Corrie ten Boom

As months went by, Corrie longed to travel and tell more people about Jesus. In 1946, she traveled all over the United States. But restlessness still filled her heart. When she had left Ravensbrück two years earlier, she had said, "I'll go anywhere God sends me, but I hope never to Germany."

Yet Corrie knew God wanted something more from her. She knew her path led to the one land she dreaded. But the nation of horror would become for her a land of blessing. For over the next decades, Corrie traveled—even across Germany—teaching how the mercy of the cross was stronger than the might of the Nazi swastika.

Corrie shared the good news of the cross all throughout Germany—from Berlin to Munich (as recounted in chapter 1). In Darmstadt, Corrie rented an abandoned concentration camp and transformed its dull gray buildings into a place of healing for the German people. Remembering Betsie's dreams, Corrie painted the buildings bright yellow-green. Like a hospital for hearts and minds, the Darmstadt rehabilitation center offered help to hurting Germans for eleven years. And Corrie consistently ministered there while continuing her other travels.

Fourteen years after her release, Corrie returned to Ravensbrück. Along with other survivors, she commemorated the lives of the 96,000 women who died there. During that visit, Corrie finally learned the

— The Swastika —

 The swastika symbol did not start with Adolf Hitler or the Nazi political party. In fact, the word *swastika* originally meant "good fortune" or "good luck." The symbol has been around for thousands of years. But Hitler adopted the symbol for his political party. The Nazis created their own flag: a black swastika symbol surrounded by a white circle on a red flag. This flag flew over Nazi-controlled countries and decorated tanks, airplanes, and military uniforms.

reason for her release: she was liberated by mistake. Someone made an error in her paperwork. A week after gaining her freedom, while she was at the hospital in Groningen, all prisoners her age had been killed.

In the years after prison, Corrie created homes—places of refuge and rest—for her friends and former enemies. But for Corrie, her place in this world had changed. Within eight years of the war ending, both Willem and Nollie had died. Corrie's home was no longer Holland. And her refuge was no longer the Beje. She later wrote, "My hiding place was now in Jesus alone." For God had called her to minister to people around the world. Secure in his protection and care and with her red suitcase in hand, Corrie followed that call across the globe.

12

The Whole World

1945–1983

AFTER WORLD WAR II, Corrie dedicated the rest of her life to talking about Jesus. She taught in jails, colleges, churches, and children's clubs. Again and again, she told everyone that Jesus can save, even in the face of evil. Jesus is victor!

Corrie even traveled to countries where religious

freedom was limited or illegal. She visited Russia, East Germany, Vietnam, China, and other Communist countries. On one of her trips, the leaders of a government-controlled church invited her to speak.

— Her Wise Father —

In her travels, Corrie often retold stories from her childhood to teach valuable lessons. Here's one such story:

As a little child, Corrie crawled under the covers at bedtime and nestled next to her sister. Nollie was a year and a half older, brave, and out-going. But Corrie was shy and often scared. She was afraid of her family leaving her, afraid of going to the doctor, and afraid of death.

One night she thought about their neighbor who had died. *If people die, that means that one day Nollie, Betsie, . . . one day they might die too*. Just then she heard her papa's footsteps on the creaking staircase. He opened the door.

"Papa, I need you!" Corrie sobbed from under the covers. "You can't die."

Papa leaned over the small bed. His long beard tickled her face. He arranged the blankets in his perfect way and sat beside her. "Corrie, when you and I take the train to Amsterdam, when do I give you the money for the ticket? Three weeks before?"

Blinking away the tears, Corrie replied, "No, Papa, you give me the money for the ticket just before we get on the train."

"Exactly. And our wise Father in heaven knows when we're going to need things too. . . . When the time comes that some of us will have to die," Papa continued, "he will supply the strength you need—just in time. Don't run out ahead of him, Corrie."

Corrie felt that the government officials saw her as "a harmless old Dutch woman." But in their crowded cathedral, she boldly taught about "the abundant life in Jesus Christ—the joy, the unspeakable love, and the peace that passes all understanding."

While visiting another restricted country, Corrie was detained at a border crossing. The Communist guard led her to a back room for questioning: "What are you doing here? What's in your suitcase? Why do you have a Bible?"

Corrie smiled, "I'm here to visit friends." Then she added, "Do you ever read the Bible?" For three hours she and the guard talked. He let her pass the checkpoint. And he wrote in his official report: "When in prison, Corrie ten Boom received from God the commission to bring the gospel of Jesus Christ over the whole world."

In her travels, Corrie also ministered to prisoners. In California, she visited the infamous San Quentin Prison. And in Africa, she visited a dreadful prison in Rwanda. Between the buildings, the prisoners sat on large leaves strewn atop warm mud, thick and foul. Like steam rising from a pot of boiling water, a haze rose from the dark smelly ground. Bugs swarmed the prisoners' mud-caked legs. Their faces betrayed their despair, hatred, and hopelessness.

Corrie thought, *What could I, an old Dutch woman, say to these miserable men that would help their lives?* She opened her Bible to Galatians 5:22: "The fruit of the Spirit is love, joy. . . ." She quietly prayed, "Joy? . . . In these surroundings, Lord?"

She scanned the group, took a breath, and began her lesson. The local missionary translated Corrie's words: "What a friend we have in him. He is always with us. When we are depressed, he gives us joy. . . . When we hate, he fills us with his forgiveness. When we are afraid, he causes us to love." Corrie told them about the horrors of Ravensbrück prison. And she testified that "the reality of God's love was just as sure as the cruelty of men."

The prisoners sat forward on their muddy mats. Some began to smile. Corrie continued, "Men, do

you know Jesus is willing to live in your hearts? He says, 'I stand at the door of your heart and knock. If anyone hears my voice and opens the door, I come in.' Just think: That same Jesus loves you and will live in your heart and give you joy in the midst of this mud." Then Corrie encouraged the men to ask Jesus to be their Savior.

As Corrie and the missionary made their way to the gates, the prisoners and guards chanted in unison. "Old woman, come back. Old woman, come back and tell us more about Jesus."

Telling people about Jesus was what Corrie loved to do. She traveled the world for thirty-three years, from Holland to Hong Kong, from Uganda to Uzbekistan, from Mexico to Moscow. She visited over sixty countries. She rode camels in Egypt and elephants in India.

And as she traveled, she also wrote books, journals, and magazine articles. She retold the stories of life in the Beje, of prison, and most importantly about Jesus. Just months after she returned home from

Ravensbrück, she published *A Prisoner and Yet*. It was her first book, and in the following years, she would write over twenty-five more books. In 1971, when Corrie was seventy-nine years old, she published her most famous work: *The Hiding Place*. Within four years, *The Hiding Place* had sold over three million copies worldwide. And in 1975, Corrie attended the debut of *The Hiding Place* movie in Beverly Hills, California.

In the years after prison, Corrie also gained recognition and received awards. In 1962, when she was seventy years old, she was knighted by Queen Juliana of the Netherlands. Six years later, Corrie was honored by Israeli Prime Minister Golda Meir in a ceremony at the Holocaust Memorial in Israel. Corrie was recognized for saving the lives of over seven hundred Jewish people.

On February 28, 1977, exactly thirty-three years after the day of her arrest, Corrie moved into a home in California. She was almost eighty-five years old, and her traveling days were over. She planned to rest and write. But a few months later, she suffered a stroke. And over the next five years, she suffered several more. Eventually she lost her ability to speak and was confined to her bed.

On April 15, 1983, Corrie died. It was her ninety-first birthday. Some Jewish people believe that to die on one's own birthday is a sign of a special blessing: the completion of God's mission for that life. She was buried in Orange County, California.

Five years after her death, the Beje opened as a museum: the Corrie ten Boom House. Visitors can sit at the dining room table, climb the winding stairs, and crawl into the hiding place.

By the end of her life, millions of people knew Corrie ten Boom's name. The daughter of a Dutch watchmaker had lived a heroic life. She helped hundreds of Jewish people and went to prison for it. She faced beatings and the threat of death. Yet like her Savior, she forgave her enemies and taught others to do the same. She dedicated her life to teach the Bible and tell everyone about Jesus.

The inscription on her gravestone summarizes what she taught. The message of a lifetime packed into one sentence. A worldwide announcement of good news in three short words:

Jesus is Victor.

Nothing could take away his victory, not war, not betrayal, not prison, and not death. Corrie had clung to her victorious Savior throughout her life. He had never let her go, and he never would, not even in death.

Lessons from a Life

IN 1947, CORRIE STOOD in a church basement in Munich, Germany. A large man with blue-gray eyes stood in front of her. His hand extended toward her. And the memories of Ravensbrück flashed through her mind.

Her whole life had led to this moment. But how can you forgive the unforgivable?

It would be the most difficult thing she would have to do. But she knew she must. *Haven't I just taught that everyone has sinned, but God will forgive those sins. And when God forgives sins, he does not remember them.*

She knew Jesus had forgiven all her sins. But how could she forgive this man standing in front of her? Corrie silently poured out her heart to the Lord: "Jesus, help me! . . . I can lift my hand. I can do that much. You supply the feeling."

Slowly she raised her hand to meet his. As his large hand enveloped hers, Corrie suddenly felt a sense of warmth and love. Her anger melted away. With tears of joy in her eyes, she exclaimed, "I forgive you, brother! . . . With all my heart!"

———

Corrie had learned to forgive. But how?

She could forgive because she believed the Bible's grand story of God's forgiveness. Her most treasured book told the true story of God's love for the people who had rejected him.

The opening pages of the Bible tell how God had created a perfect world, but people chose to go their own way. And sin and death came into the story.

And like a towering prison wall, sin separated people from God. But God loved people so much that he made a way to tear down the wall. First Peter 3:18 states, "For Christ also suffered once for sins, the righteous for the unrighteous, that he might bring us to God." Jesus, God's Son, came to earth and lived a perfect life. But in great injustice, he was hated, arrested, beaten, and killed on a cross. He didn't deserve to die. He had lived a perfect life. But Jesus willingly died as a common criminal.

His death paid the penalty of sin—not his own, but the sins of others. Because sin had been paid for, Jesus's death tore down the wall between God and those who turn to him. And he brought forgiveness and life with him forever. John 3:16 says, "For God so loved the world, that he gave his only Son, that whoever believes in him should not perish but have eternal life."

By sending his Son to die, God had shown Corrie how to love and how to forgive. She had been forgiven. And because of Jesus, she could now also forgive others. "We love because he first loved us" (1 John 4:19).

Corrie's life story had been full of family and friends, and then war, tragedy, and loss. She was an ordinary person thrown into extraordinary pain.

Yet by the end of her life, Corrie ten Boom was one of the most beloved Christians in the world. Millions knew her name and her story, and thousands had come to know her God. And many who came to hear her, came with a question: How do you learn to forgive?

The answer, they learned, had the power to change everything about them. Corrie knew it was true.

God's forgiveness had transformed her life.

Study Questions

Chapter 1: The Face in the Crowd

1. What was the topic of Corrie's lesson at the church in Munich?

2. Who was the man that approached Corrie?

3. Why did the man ask for Corrie's forgiveness?

Chapter 2: Small Beginnings

1. Why did Corrie's family pray for her when she was born?

2. How did Corrie feel about going to her first day of school? Who helped her on her first day of school?

Have you ever been afraid to try something new? Explain what helped you to be brave.

3. What nickname did her family call their house and watch shop?

4. Name one of the groups of people that Corrie prayed for as a little girl.

Chapter 3: Being a Somebody

1. Compare Corrie's life as a nanny to her life at the Beje. What did she realize she missed after becoming a nanny?

2. Why did the Ten Boom family bring German children into their home? What was happening in Germany at that time?

3. What major accomplishment did Corrie achieve by the time she was thirty-two years old? Why was this significant in Holland?

Chapter 4: The Invasion

1. After the invasion, the German government forced restrictions on radios, telephones, and newspapers. Why do you think that the Nazis forced these restrictions on the Dutch citizens?

2. What signs did Corrie and her father see the Nazis posting all around Haarlem? What other changes happened to the Jews in Holland?

3. Why do you think the Underground movement got its name?

Chapter 5: Ration Cards

1. Why did Corrie need more ration cards? Why couldn't the visitors at the Beje get their own cards?

2. Corrie went to her big brother Willem to ask for help. Why couldn't he help Corrie?

3. How did Corrie feel about Willem's suggestion about getting ration cards?

4. Corrie went to see Fred. Where did he work? And what plan did Fred devise to get ration cards?

Chapter 6: The Secret Room

1. The Dutch Underground workers used the same last name. What was the name? Why do you think they use this name?

2. How did the Underground workers bring building supplies to the Beje?

3. Why would the Beje need a hiding place for the Jews and the other guests staying there?

4. Why did Mr. Smit laugh with delight as he climbed the stairs in the Beje? Why did he want the hiding place to be located in Corrie's room?

Chapter 7: Jesus Is Victor

1. What did the Ten Booms call their resistance group? What activities did they participate in?

2. What term describes the young Dutchmen who hid during the war? Why were they hiding?

3. In this chapter, what did Corrie say was the "hardest thing she had done"? Why was this hard?

4. What phrase was written on the plaque on the wall? How did this phrase help Corrie during the time of her arrest?

Chapter 8: Light in the Darkness

1. What did the nurse give to Corrie when she first entered the prison at Scheveningen?

2. How did Corrie know to look under the stamp? What message did she find? What did it mean?

3. Why did Corrie call out for the guard? What lesson did God teach Corrie from the guard's heartless response? Can you think of a time when someone treated you unkindly when you were sad? How did you handle that feeling?

Chapter 9: Fear and Forgiveness

1. What was Corrie's main job at the Philips factory? Why did she get this job?

2. Corrie was angry at the man who betrayed her family. At first, she did not want to forgive him. What helped Corrie forgive him? Can you think of a time in your life when you didn't want to forgive? How did you handle that feeling?

3. Corrie compared her life to a tapestry. What does it mean that God was weaving a beautiful picture in the tapestry? Why did she say that her life felt like tangled strings?

4. Compare Corrie's prison experience at Scheveningen Prison to her experience at Vught Prison. What were the differences? Which do you feel was better?

Chapter 10: Ravensbrück

1. Describe how Corrie smuggled the Bible and sweater into the camp. Why was she not searched?

2. What did Corrie not want to thank God for when she first came to Ravensbrück? What helped her change her mind?

3. How did Corrie react when the guard beat Betsie?

4. Before she died, Betsie told Corrie about her dreams for their lives after prison. Describe the two ministries that Betsie wanted to start in the future. How did she envision these two places would look?

Chapter 11: Home

1. Corrie spent ten days at the hospital in Groningen. Name three things that Corrie enjoyed while at the hospital. Why did she enjoy these so much?

2. After Corrie forgave the man who had betrayed her family, what did she want him to do?

3. What group of people did Corrie invite to stay at the Beje? What is the difference between these people and the people who stayed at the Beje during the war? How would you feel if you had the choice to open your home to people like this?

4. What country did Corrie say she hoped she would never have to travel to again? What helped her overcome this wish? What did Corrie establish in Darmstadt?

5. Corrie went to Ravensbrück fourteen years after she was released from prison. What did she find out about her release?

Chapter 12: The Whole World

1. What was the topic of Corrie's lesson when she visited the prison in Rwanda? How did the prisoners respond to her lesson?

2. Why do you think Corrie purposefully visited prisons around the world? Why might the prisoners have been willing to listen to her teaching?

3. Name the two world leaders who honored Corrie.

4. What is the name of Corrie's most famous book about her life?

5. How old was Corrie when she died? What did some people consider special about her dying on April 15?

Conclusion: Lessons from a Life

1. Imagine you were Corrie ten Boom. What might you have said or done to your former prison guard? How was Corrie able to forgive him?

2. In your own words, explain how sin is like a prison wall that separates people from God. What is the only way to tear down that wall?

3. What had transformed Corrie's life?

Timeline

CORRIE TEN BOOM'S LIFE
AND WORLD EVENTS

Year	Events	Age
1837	Corrie's grandfather Willem ten Boom opens the Ten Boom Watch Shop.	
1844	Willem ten Boom begins praying for the Jewish people.	
1889	Dutch artist Vincent van Gogh paints *The Starry Night*.	
1892	On April 15, Corrie is born in Amsterdam, the Netherlands, on Good Friday.	0
1893	Amsterdam hosts the first official world championships in speed skating.	1
1897	Corrie's family moves into the Beje. Corrie becomes a Christian.	5

☐ CORRIE TEN BOOM'S LIFE ▨ WORLD EVENTS

Year	Events	Age
1903	On December 17, Orville and Wilbur Wright fly the first successful engine-powered flight at Kitty Hawk, North Carolina, USA.	11
1911	Corrie becomes a nanny. Corrie's Aunt Bep dies of tuberculosis.	19
1914	Babe Ruth begins his major league baseball career with the Boston Red Sox. On July 28, World War I begins.	22
1916	On August 23, Corrie's brother Willem marries Christina "Tine" van Veen.	24
1919	On July 23, Corrie's sister Nollie marries Frederik "Flip" van Woerden. Corrie's Aunt Jans dies from diabetes.	27
1921	On October 17, Corrie's mother Cornelia "Cor" Johanna Arnolda Luitingh ten Boom dies.	29
1924	Corrie becomes the first woman licensed as a watchmaker in the Netherlands.	32
1925	The Ten Booms house missionary children. Corrie begins the Church Walk Club (which continues until 1940). On March 7, Corrie's Aunt Anna dies.	33
1933	On January 30, Adolf Hitler becomes the chancellor of Germany. On December 17, the Chicago Bears and the New York Giants football teams play in the first NFL championship game.	41

Year	Events	Age
1935	On September 15, the Nuremberg Laws remove the citizenship from German Jews and forbid Jews from marrying non-Jews in Germany.	43
1936	African-American runner Jesse Owens wins four gold medals and sets three new track records at the Berlin Summer Olympics while Adolf Hitler watched.	44
1940	Cartoon characters Tom and Jerry, Bugs Bunny, and Woody Woodpecker all make their first appearances in animated cartoons. On May 10, the German Army invades Holland.	48
1943	The Ten Booms begin sheltering Jews at the Beje. The Dutch Underground workers build the secret room.	51
1944	On February 28, the Gestapo raid the Beje and arrest the Ten Boom family. On February 29, the Ten Boom family is taken to Scheveningen Prison. On March 9, Corrie's father, Casper ten Boom, dies. On June 6, Corrie and Betsie are sent to Vught Prison.	52
1944	On June 6, Allied Armed Forces launch "Operation Overlord" invading Europe at Normandy, France. On August 4, Anne Frank and her family are arrested.	52

Year	Events	Age
1944 *(cont'd)*	On September 4, Corrie and Betsie are sent to Ravensbrück Concentration Camp, Germany.	52
	On December 16, Betsie dies at Ravensbrück.	
	On December 30, Corrie is released from prison.	
1945	On April 30, Adolf Hitler dies in Berlin, Germany.	53
	On May 5, German General Johannes Blaskowitz surrenders to Canadian General Charles Foulkes, ending the Nazi occupation of the Netherlands.	
	On September 2, WWII ends when Japan surrenders to the Allies.	
1945	In May, Corrie opens a rehabilitation home in Bloemendaal.	53
	On June 19, Corrie writes a letter to Jan Vogel saying that she forgives him.	
	In June, Corrie publishes her autobiography *Gevangene en Toch* (*A Prisoner and Yet*).	
1946	Corrie begins her ministry of traveling the world. She ministers in New York; Vermont; Washington, DC; Pennsylvania; Michigan; Illinois; Iowa; Utah; California; and Canada.	54
	On December 13, Corrie's brother Willem dies of tuberculosis, which he contracted while he was in prison.	

Year	Events	Age
1948	Princess Juliana is crowned Queen of the Netherlands. Dutch artist M. C. Escher creates *Drawing Hands*. On May 14, the State of Israel is established.	56
1949	Corrie visits the USA, Switzerland, and Germany. While in Germany, she opens the rehabilitation center at the former concentration camp in Darmstadt.	57
1950	In Great Britain, C. S. Lewis publishes *The Lion, the Witch, and the Wardrobe*.	58
1953	Corrie travels to Spain, South Africa, New Zealand, Australia, the Philippines, and Taiwan. Corrie publishes her second book, *Amazing Love*. On October 22, Corrie's sister Nollie dies.	61
1957	On October 4, the Soviet Union launches the first satellite, *Sputnik*.	65
1959	Corrie and other former prisoners return to Ravensbrück Concentration Camp for a memorial service. Corrie travels to Vietnam, Hong Kong, and throughout Europe.	67
1962	On April 17, Corrie is knighted by Dutch Queen Juliana.	70
1963	Martin Luther King Jr. gives his "I Have a Dream" speech in the USA.	71

Year	Events	Age
1965	Corrie visits the African countries of Kenya, Burundi, Rwanda, Tanzania, Uganda, and Congo. In Rwanda, Corrie ministers in a prison.	73
1968	On February 28, Corrie travels to Israel where she is honored because of the Jewish lives she saved during WWII. Corrie ministers in the USA, Great Britain, the Netherlands, Germany, and Russia.	76
1971	Corrie's most famous book, *The Hiding Place*, is published.	79
1975	On September 29, Corrie attends the debut of *The Hiding Place* movie in Beverly Hills, California. In November, Corrie publishes her *Prison Letters*.	83
1977	On February 28, Corrie retires to Placentia, California. On September 25, Corrie visits San Quentin Prison in California.	85
1980	On February 22, the United States hockey team defeats the Soviet Union in the "Miracle on Ice" game at the Lake Placid Winter Olympic Games. On April 30, Princess Beatrix becomes Queen of the Netherlands. On May 22, Namco Limited introduces the arcade game *Pac-Man*.	90

Year	Events	Age
1983	Nintendo releases the first *Mario Bros.* arcade game. McDonald's offers the Chicken McNugget for the first time in their restaurants worldwide. Motorola develops the first commercially available cell phone.	91
1983	Corrie suffers a stroke. On April 15, Corrie dies on her birthday. She is buried in the Fairhaven Memorial Park in Santa Ana, California.	91
1988	The Beje is reopened as the Corrie ten Boom House Museum.	

More to Explore

IF YOU'D LIKE TO READ MORE about Corrie ten Boom, there are several books that tell the story of her life. Some of the books in the list below are written for young readers like you. Some of the adult books in the list are challenging to read but worth the effort.

BOOKS TO TRY NEXT

Janet and Geoff Benge. *Corrie ten Boom: Keeper of the Angels' Den*. Seattle, WA: YWAM, 1999. A chapter book overview of Corrie ten Boom's life.

Lonnie Hull DuPont, Corrie ten Boom, Elizabeth Sherrill, and John Sherrill. *The Hiding Place*. Young Reader's Edition. Minneapolis: Chosen, 2015. A simplified edition of the famous book telling the story of Corrie ten Boom's life during World War II and her imprisonment.

Renee Taft Meloche. *Corrie ten Boom: Shining in the Darkness*. Seattle, WA: YWAM, 2002. A short, illustrated overview of Corrie ten Boom's life story written in the form of a poem.

ADULT BOOKS YOU MIGHT ENJOY

Corrie ten Boom. *A Prisoner and Yet*. 1947. Reprint, Fort Washington, PA: CLC, 2022. Written months after her release from prison, this book gives Corrie ten Boom's first-hand account of the months she spent in prison.

Corrie ten Boom with Jamie Buckingham. *Tramp for the Lord*. 1974. Reprint, Fort Washington, PA: CLC, 1974. In this book, Corrie ten Boom relates stories of her travels in the decades after her release from prison.

Corrie ten Boom with Carole C. Carlson. *In My Father's House*. 1976. Reprint, Roseburg, OR: Lighthouse Trails, 2011. In this book, Corrie ten Boom tells the story of her life leading up to World War II.

Corrie ten Boom, John L. Sherrill, and Elizabeth Sherrill. *The Hiding Place*. 1971. Reprint, Grand

Rapids, MI: Chosen, 2006. Corrie's most famous book tells her story of working with the Dutch Underground during World War II and her dire experiences in Nazi concentration camps.

Larry Loftis. *The Watchmaker's Daughter: The True Story of World War II Heroine Corrie ten Boom.* New York: HarperCollins, 2023. Written from a secular perspective, this book provides a full biography of Corrie ten Boom's life in the context of historical world events.

A Note on Sources

THE LANGUAGE in some quotations has been modernized. Also, while every effort has been made to ensure historical accuracy, some instances of dialogue in this biography represent creative reconstructions. Although such dialogue is not documented in the historical record, the author has sought to reflect the context, people, and available sources as accurately as possible.

The following books and other resources were used as sources in the research and writing of this biography.

Carlson, Carole C. *Corrie ten Boom: Her Life, Her Faith.* Fleming H. Revell, 1983.

CityDesk. "Gezellig—a Word That Encompasses the Heart of Dutch Culture." *Amsterdam Tourist Information* (blog), April 20, 2007. https://www.dutch amsterdam.nl.

Dictionary.com. "Why Are People from the Netherlands Called Dutch?" December 16, 2011. https://www.dictionary.com.

"The History of the Swastika." In *Holocaust Encyclopedia*. United States Holocaust Memorial Meseum. Accessed October 12, 2023. https://encyclopedia.ushmm.org.

"Gezellig." In Cambridge Dictionary: Translate Dutch to English. Accessed October 20, 2023. https://dictionary.cambridge.org.

"Is 'Holland' the Same Place as 'the Netherlands'?" In *Britannica*. Accessed October 16, 2023. https://www.britannica.com.

Loftis, Larry. *The Watchmaker's Daughter: The True Story of World War II Heroine Corrie ten Boom.* HarperCollins Publishers, 2023.

Moore, Pam Rosewell. *Life Lessons from the Hiding Place: Discovering the Heart of Corrie ten Boom.* Chosen Books, 2004.

"Netherlands: Bicycle Fleet | Statista." Accessed October 20, 2023. https://www.statista.com/statistics.

"Operation Manna-Chowhound: Deliverance from Above." The National WWII Museum, New Orleans. May 6, 2020. https://www.nationalww2 museum.org.

Rijk, Marian. "Headwind, Tailwind. How the Bicycle Became a Dutch Symbol." Translated by Anna Asbury. *The Low Countries*. July 2, 2020. https://www .the-low-countries.com.

ten Boom, Corrie. *Amazing Love: True Stories of the Power of Forgiveness*. Originally published in 1953. CLC Publications, 2022.

ten Boom, Corrie. *Clippings from My Notebook*. World Wide Publications, 1982.

ten Boom, Corrie. *Corrie ten Boom's Prison Letters*. Originally published in 1975. CLC Publications, 2022.

ten Boom, Corrie. *God Is My Hiding Place*. Chosen Books, 2021.

ten Boom, Corrie, with John L. Sherrill and Elizabeth Sherrill. *The Hiding Place*. Originally published in 1971. Chosen Books, 2006.

ten Boom, Corrie, with Carole C. Carlson. *In My Father's House*. Originally published in 1976. Lighthouse Trails Publishing, 2011.

ten Boom, Corrie. *A Prisoner and Yet.* Originally published in 1947. CLC Publications, 2022.

ten Boom, Corrie, with Jamie Buckingham. *Tramp for the Lord.* Originally published in 1974. CLC Publications, 2023.

Also Available from the Lives of Faith and Grace Series

Perfect for summer reading—or all year round—the Lives of Faith and Grace series will engage middle-grade readers (ages 8–13) with the real-life stories of Christian men and women from history.

For more information, visit **crossway.org**.